GOLDEN WORDS UPON GOLDEN WORDS...FOR EVERY MUSLIM.

"Imaam al-Barbahaaree, may Allaah have mercy upon him said:

May Allaah have mercy upon you! Examine carefully the speech of everyone you hear from in your time particularly. So do not act in haste and do not enter into anything from it until you ask and see: Did any of the Companions of the Prophet, may Allaah's praise and salutations be upon him, speak about it, or did any of the scholars? So if you find a narration from them about it, cling to it, do not go beyond it for anything and do not give precedence to anything over it and thus fall into the Fire.

Explanation by Sheikh Saaleh al-Fauzaan, may Allaah preserve him:

'Do not be hasty in accepting as correct what you may hear from the people especially in these later times. As now there are many who speak about so many various matters, issuing rulings and ascribing to themselves both knowledge and the right to speak. This is especially the case after the emergence and spread of new modern day media technologies.

S uch that everyone now can speak and bring forth that which is in truth worthless; by this meaning words of no true value - speaking about whatever they wish in the name of knowledge and in the name of the religion of Islaam. It has even reached the point that you find the people of misguidance and the members of the various groups of misguidance and deviance from the religion speaking as well. Such individuals have now become those who speak in the name of the religion of Islaam through means such as the various satellite television channels. Therefore be very cautious!

It is upon you oh Muslim, and upon you oh student of knowledge individually, to verify matters and not rush to embrace everything and anything you may hear. It is upon you to verify the truth of what you hear, asking, 'Who else also makes this same statement or claim?', 'Where did this thought or concept originate or come from?', 'Who is its reference or source authority?'. Asking what are the evidences which support it from within the Book and the Sunnah? And inquiring where has the individual who is putting this forth studied and taken his knowledge from? From who has he studied the knowledge of Islaam?

Each of these matters requires verification through inquiry and investigation, especially in the present age and time. As it is not every speaker who should rightly be considered a source of knowledge, even if he is well spoken and eloquent, and can manipulate words captivating his listeners. Do not be taken in and accept him until you are aware of the degree and scope of what he possesses of knowledge and understanding. As perhaps someone's words may be few, but possess true understanding, and perhaps another will have a great deal of speech yet he is actually ignorant to such a degree that he doesn't actually posses anything of true understanding. Rather he only has the ability to enchant with his speech so that the people are deceived. Yet he puts forth the perception that he is a scholar, that he is someone of true understanding and comprehension, that he is a capable thinker, and so forth. Through such means and ways he is able to deceive and beguile the people, taking them away from the way of truth.

Thereforewhatistobegiventrueconsideration is not the amount of the speech put forth or that one can extensively discuss a subject. Rather the criterion that is to be given consideration is what that speech contains within it of sound authentic knowledge, what it contains of the established and transmitted principles of Islaam. As perhaps a short or brief statement which is connected to or has a foundation in the established principles can be of greater benefit than a great deal of speech which simply rambles on, and through hearing you don't actually receive very much benefit from.

This is the reality which is present in our time; one sees a tremendous amount of speech which only possesses within it a small amount of actual knowledge. We see the presence of many speakers yet few people of true understanding and comprehension.' "

[The eminent major scholar Sheikh Saaleh al-Fauzaan, may Allaah preserve him- 'A Valued Gift for the Reader Of Comments Upon the Book Sharh as-Sunnah', page 102-103]

This pocket edition is based upon appendices taken from the larger book:

Foundations For The New Muslim & Newly Striving Muslim

A Short Journey Selected Questions & Answers With
Sheikh 'Abdul-'Azeez Ibn 'Abdullah Ibn Baaz

[Book 4 - 30 Days of Guidance Series]

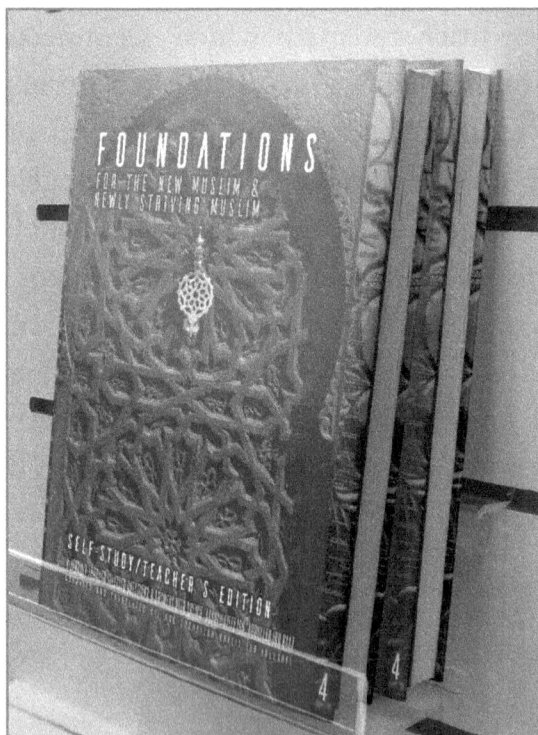

The original course book is intended for both the person who has newly embraced Islaam or that Muslim or Muslimah whom Allaah has blessed to now have the resolve within themselves to truly turn towards their Most Merciful Lord and commit themselves to becoming a better worshipper upon knowledge. It for that individual who, regardless of the direction they came from, wishes to change both the inward and outward aspects of their lives to now move in a direction truly pleasing to Allaah.

It discusses: *What are the conditions of correct Islaam? Is faith only what is in our hearts? When is it necessary for me to ask a scholar? What is the guidance of Islaam about our health? What should I do after falling into sin again and again? Do I have to make up for my previous negligence? How should I interact with the non-Muslims I know?* and more...

Collected and Translated
by Abu Sukhailah Khalil Ibn-Abelahyi al-Amreekee

[Available: **Now** ¦ pages: **400+**
price: (Soft cover) **$27.5**
(Hard cover) **$45**
(eBook) **$9.99**]

CATEGORIES OF KNOWLEDGE, CLEAR PRINCIPLES, BENEFITS, & GUIDING ADVICE

LET THE SCHOLARS SPEAK- CLARITY & GUIDANCE (BOOK 2)

Translated & Compiled By
Abu Sukhailah Khalil Ibn-Abelahyi

Table of Contents

AMENDED INTRODUCTION

In the name of Allaah, The Most Gracious, The Most Merciful

Verily, all praise is due to Allaah, we praise Him, we seek His assistance and we ask for His forgiveness. We seek refuge in Him from the evils of our souls and the evils of our actions. Whoever Allaah guides, no one can lead him astray and whoever is caused to go astray, there is no one that can guide him. I bear witness that there is no deity worthy of worship except Allaah alone with no partners. And I bear witness that Muhammad is His worshipper and Messenger.

❧ *Oh you who believe, fear Allaah as He ought to be feared and do not die except while you are Muslims.* ❧-(Surah Aal-'Imraan:102)

❧ *Oh mankind, fear Allaah who created you from a single soul and from that, He created its mate. And from them He brought forth many men and women. And fear Allaah to whom you demand your mutual rights. Verily, Allaah is an ever All-Watcher over you.* ❧-(Surah an-Nisaa:1)

❧ *Oh you who believe, fear Allaah and speak a word that is truthful (and to the point) - He will rectify your deeds and forgive you your sins. And whoever obeys Allaah and His Messenger has achieved a great success.* ❧-(Surah al-Ahzaab:70-71)

As for what follows:

The Messenger of Allaah, who was sent as a mercy to all mankind, cultivated and nurtured the best of generations upon both entering Islaam and committing themselves to fully living the guidance of Islaam. He showed that the revealed guidance of Islaam is what enables true success both now as well as in the Hereafter. It is narrated in Saheeh Muslim that Abu Maalik Ashaja'ee narrated on the authority of his father that whenever a person embraced Islaam, the Messenger of Allaah, may the praise and salutations of Allaah be upon him, instructed him to say the following supplication:[1]

{O Allaah, forgive me, have mercy upon me, direct me to the path of righteousness and provide me with sustenance}

اللَّهُمَّ اغْفِرْلِي وَارْحَمْنِي وَاهْدِنِي وَارْزُقْنِي

Likewise, for that Muslim who has recommitted himself to following the guidance of Islaam, he should know that the Messenger of Allaah, may the praise and salutations of Allaah be upon him, also mentioned a similar supplication. When asked by a Muslim who wanted to truly understand and implement properly supplicating to and asking from Allaah of what would benefit him, he was informed of the following supplication. It is narrated in Sunan Ibn Maajah that Abu Maalik Sa'd bin Tariq, narrated from his father that a man had come to the Messenger of Allaah, and he heard him say,[2]

---

[1] Saheeh Muslim:2697

[2] Sunan Ibn Maajah: 3845- this narration was authenticated by Sheikh al-Albaanee in his verification of Sunan Ibn Maajah, as well as within Silsilat al-Hadeeth as-Saheehah no. 1318. It is narrated by al-Haakim in his work al-Mustadrak: vol. 1 no. 529, Imaam Ahmad in his Musnad in narrations 16122, 16126 & others, Ibn Abee Shaybah in his work al-Mussanaf: narration 29 &798, Saheeh Ibn Khuzaaymah in narrations 726 & 821, and other reliable sources including al-Adaab al-Mufrad of Imaam al-Bukhaaree: 651 (where it is also authenticated by Sheikh al-Albaanee, may Allaah have mercy upon him) with the wording which means, "*People both men and women used to visit the Prophet, may the praise and salutations of Allaah be upon him and*

"O Messenger of Allaah, what should I say when I ask of Allaah?" He said:

{Say: O Allaah, forgive me, have mercy on me, keep me safe and sound and grant me provision)

اللَّهُمَّ اغْفِرْلِي وَارْحَمْنِي وَعَافِنِي وَارْزُقْنِي

and he held up his four fingers apart from the thumb and said: These combine your religious and worldly affairs.}

A related reminder comes from Sheikh as-Sa'dee, may Allaah have mercy upon him, who said,[3]

"From the most beneficial of what may be noted about seeking and realizing good in ones future affairs is using the following supplication which the Prophet used to supplicate with: {O Allaah, make upright my religion so that all my affairs are protected, set right for me my worldly matters where my life presently exists, make good for me my Hereafter which is my final home to which I have to return, and facilitate in my life the performing of all types of good, and make death a comfort for me by closing the door to every evil.}

Similar to this is his statement about supplication for those encountering difficulties, {O Allaah! Thy mercy is what I hope for, so do not abandon me to myself for an instant, but put all my affairs in good order for me. There is none worthy of worship except You alone.}

If a worshiper of Allaah perseveres in making these supplications which encompass what rectifies his future affairs in from both the aspect of his practice of the religion and in his worldly matters, with an attentive focused heart, a true pure intention, and with those actions which help realize that good, Allaah will make a

---

ask ' Messenger of Allaah, what should we say when we supplicate?...'
[3]   al-Wassa'il al-Mufeedah lil Hayyat as-Sa'eedah

12

reality these matters which he supplicated for, hoped for and worked towards, and change his condition to be one of happiness and contentment."

This course book is intended for both the person who has embraced Islaam, whether recently or some time ago, as well as that Muslim or Muslimah whom Allaah has blessed to have the resolve within themselves to now truly turn towards their Most Merciful Lord and commit themselves to becoming a better worshipper. It for that individual who, regardless of the direction they came from, wishes to change both the inward and outward aspects of their lives to now move in a direction truly pleasing to Allaah, by establishing a strong connection to His revealed guidance as well as the principles and people of that guidance. The material is based upon selected beneficial responses to questions, and statements of guidance from one of the leading scholars of our century and age, Sheikh 'Abdul-'Azeez Ibn 'Abdullah Ibn Baaz, may Allaah have abundant mercy upon him. I pray that by Allaah's permission it will aid and assist both the new Muslim and the newly committed Muslim in fully realizing the blessing of Islaam they have been personally granted and favored with and chosen as individuals, bringing success in this world and the next. As there is no doubt that as Sheikh al-Islaam Ibn Taymeeyah, may Allaah have mercy upon him, said,[4]

"Our revealed Book, our Prophet, our religion, our Ummah, is better than any other book, religion, prophet, or nation. Therefore you should thank Allaah for what He has blessed you with."

We must take and use the incredible blessing we have in Islaam and strengthen our connection to our Lord and His chosen path and way of life, and furthermore protect it from what would harm it or stifle its growth within our individual lives Maalik ibn Dinar, may Allaah have mercy

[4]   Majmu'a al-Fataawa vol. 28 pg. 411

on him, is reported to have said:

> *"Faith or our emaan begins in the heart weak and feeble like a sprout or seedling. If its owner takes care of it and nourishes it with portions of beneficial knowledge and righteous deeds, and keeps away from it overshadowing weeds and things that will make it weak, it will soon grow and expand. It will develop in both its roots and branches, and then bear fruit and provide continual shade, until it becomes like a mountain. But if its owner neglects it and does not take care of it, then like a plant seedling, a goat may come and eat it, or a child might come and pluck it out, or the weeds around it will grow and overshadow it until they cause it wither away. Our emaan is the same way."*

Similarly Khaythamah ibn 'Abd al-Rahmaan, may Allaah have mercy on him, said,[5]

> *"Faith grows strong in fertile soil and grows weak in arid soil. Its fertile soil is righteous deeds and its arid soil is sin and disobedience."*

The road to our success as Muslims individually, and as an Ummah is simple and clear if we turn towards and take firm hold of the enduring guidance we have been sent, but this clarity does not mean that the road is easy or without any difficulty. One matter that may help a new Muslim, is knowing that Allaah has a specific role for them in their truly aiding and helping Islaam. As it is affirmed as Allaah's way to bring new people into Islaam to support and establish his religion. It is narrated in Sunan Ibn Maajah and the Musnad of Imaam Ahmad, that Bakr bin Zur'ah narrated to us saying: "I heard Abu 'Inabah Al-Khawlaanee, who had prayed facing both prayer directions of ritual prayer with the Messenger of Allaah, may Allaah's praise and salutations be upon him,

---

[5]   Both statements quoted by Ibn Taymeeyah in mentioned in the work Kitaab al-Eemaan, p. 213

say: 'I heard the Messenger of Allaah, may Allaah's praise and salutations be upon him, say *{Allaah will continue to cultivate new people in this religion and utilize them in His obedience.}* Sheikh al-Albaanee, may Allaah have mercy upon him, authenticated this narration and explained it meaning in the context of other authentic narrations saying,[6]

> *"Regarding this hadeeth narration, the least grade of authenticity it can be said that it is an authentic narration of a good level, meaning that it is accepted, and taken as hadeeth we are guided by. It states, {Allaah will continue to cultivate new people in this religion and utilize them in His obedience.} will continue, meaning continue until the end of time here on earth.*
>
> *Yet a person when he hears the authentic narration {There will not come an age except that the age that comes after it will be more severe in the evil which is found.} may feel some hopelessness. However if you look at the current situation of the world even after fourteen centuries have passed, you find that there are undoubtedly good people present. Then how can we truthfully state, {There will not come an age except that the age that comes after it will be more sever in the evil which is found.} but also say that goodness and righteous people will always remain until the Day of Resurrection? In fact, we say and affirm that {Allaah will continue to cultivate new people in this religion and utilize them in His obedience.} since the presence of righteous people within the Muslim Ummah will never cease until the Day of Resurrection.*
>
> *There will never stop being a group from within the Muslim Ummah standing upon the truth, successful*

[6]   This narration is authentic as mentioned under narration number 2442 in the work Silsilaat al-Hadeeth as-Saheehah

*and victorious upon it.[7] As such this hadeeth narration when considered alongside to the narration {**There will not come an age except that the age that comes after it will be more sever in the evil which is found.**} indicates that the second narration about evil is general in meaning, meaning that it is a general assessment of ages and periods of history. Such that in regard to viewing the majority of people in the world you will need a continuing decrease in the people of goodness among them. Yet there will always be among them righteous individuals. Therefore the meaning of the hadeeth about each age being more evil that the one previous to it, does not mean that all goodness will be absent completely, no. Rather righteousness is always present in the Ummah of Muhammad until the Day of Resurrection just as is stated in this hadeeth {**Allaah will continue to cultivate new people in this religion and utilize them in His obedience.**}. It means that some of the righteous will always be there.*

Thirty years ago, in regards to the youth for example, their previous level in gaining knowledge is not the same as the level presently witnessed. This is something we have experienced and witnessed directly, those with knowledge were much less then by a significant amount than today. At that time there were certainly some individuals, there were perhaps tens of young people who possessed strong knowledge. They unquestionably had genuine substantive knowledge that merited some of them be described as scholars. Yet still it was not the significantly increased numbers of people that we see and witness today. If previously there where tens of youth with

---

[7]   The scholar Sheikh 'Abdullah Ibn 'Abdur-Rahman Abaa Bateen, may Allaah have mercy upon him, commented on the hadeeth *{There will never cease to be a group from my Ummah manifest upon the truth.}* "What is intended by manifest is not always victorious with weapons or in battle, but rather always victorious with the knowledge based proofs and evidences, and sometimes victorious with arms and weapons." ad-Durur as-Sunneeyah fee al-Ajweebat an-Najdeeyah vol.10 pg 399

knowledge, now there are a thousand, and all praise is due to Allaah. By Allaah, the Most Exalted, the Most Magnificent, continues to cultivate new people in this religion and utilize them in His obedience.

Despite this when we examine them from another angle we find that from one aspect goodness is deficient among them, while it has increased from another angle. It has increased from the direction or angle of their desire, gaining of, and gaining a foundation in beneficial knowledge, however from the other direction, that of deeds and implementation, it is now deficient.

Can we compare the humility found among the seekers of knowledge today to that greater humility found among them thirty years ago? No, in light of our general experience. Yet this is something that increases and decreases from one aspect without including another different aspect, and varies from one land to another, and it will even be seen in one area as distinct from another, or generally recognized somewhere in respect to one aspect of goodness and righteousness while being absent from another."

Each of us should recognize daily how significant is the blessing that Allaah has chosen you as an individual to help strengthen Islaam, even if just by working to be a quiet example of a striving worshipper. How significant is the impact of each individual worshipping Allaah alone with no partners, helping guide humanity to what pleases Him and is good for them in this world and the next, by starting with ourselves and then proceeding further, just as the first Muslim community in Medinah did. The scholars of Islaam have noted the incredible effect the treaty of al-Hudaybeeyah had upon the growth of Islaam due to the non-Muslims having the chance to interact, hear and see the message of Islaam from the sincere Muslims among them. For that reason it is very important for the new Muslim and the newly committed Muslim to understand properly how to look forward and not worry about what has passed that you cannot change, nor that which your Lord, in His tremendous mercy, wiped away either through your entering Islaam or your sincere repentance from being neglectful as a worshipper. Remember as Imaam as-Sa'dee, may Allaah have mercy upon him said,[8]

"Do not be sorry about those difficult days which have passed and the situations that were not decreed for you to avoid, whether from poor health, the loss of wealth, or simply difficulty in working in worldly endeavors and what is similar to this. Instead make what you focus on and give importance to rectifying what you are doing with your day today, as a human being is in fact a child of their present day. So you shouldn't be unduly grieved about what has happened in the past, nor should you be unduly focused on looking towards what the future may possibly bring- beyond a degree which is actually beneficial for you.

You should form a good intention for and have a commitment to living up to what is correct and keeping one's promises and acting with fairness in all of your various dealing and interactions now. You should be committed to giving everything what it's due with a calm confident perspective built upon a sincere truthful faith in Allaah.

Moreover, focus upon your own shortcomings and affairs that can be improved rather than focusing upon the faults and affairs of other people generally. This approach applies to everyone, the young and old, both men and women, the societal authorities as well as those general people whom they are responsible for. They should all be

[8]   Majmu'a Mu'alifaat as-Sa'adee vol. 21 pg. 258

all working toward their betterment as is suitable for their specific situation.

Furthermore, you should be good natured and compassionate generally to all others even to animals, since Allaah is merciful to His created worshipers who show mercy to others in creation. So be prudent in all of your affairs, and open your mind to benefiting from every beneficial lesson or reminder you encounter whether connected to your worldly affairs or to our religion."

THE MANY CHALLENGES THE ROAD AHEAD HOLDS

The Permanent Committee for Scholarly Research and Ifta' was asked,[9] ***"Does a new Muslim have to perform the obligations that are prescribed for Muslims in the period between being convinced about the truth of Islaam and officially declaring and making his Islaam public?"*** They responded,

"When an individual embraces Islam, they are obligated to learn what is legislated for them, gradually, according to their ability, and to act upon this, from the initial time they are convinced that Islaam is the truth."

There are undoubtedly obstacles faced by a new Muslim as well as the newly committed Muslim in learning and practicing. Some of them are external and from the society around him, while others are internal and from within him. Among them are numerous misconceptions and false ideas spread and common in society which must be fought against as Shaytaan uses them to try and distance you away from Islaam and weaken your connection to its path of guidance. There are those who will deceptively

---

[9] Third question from ruling no. 6348 vol. 3 , pg. 388- The Permanent Committee for Scholarly Research and Ifta'

say [Why would you give up your freedom, to become a Muslim?] But we should respond as the noble Sheikh Saaleh Ibn Fauzaan, may Allaah preserve him, said,[10]

> *"True freedom is obtained through obeying the guidance of Allaah. It is not freedom to simply follow one's personal wants and desires haphazardly, this is only a submission to one's inner wants, and is not actually freedom."*

Shaytaan also tries to sow misconceptions about the value of Islaam and its suitability for the modern age, especially for those coming from countries where Muslims are a minority. Sheikh Muhammad Baazmool, explains the weakness of this claim stating,[11]

> *"What is our position towards civilization and development? There is not any matter in the Sharee'ah that stands between a Muslim and between civilization and development, nor anything that prevents a Muslim from taking those steps which advance material progress. Certainly our religion does not prevent us from those matters which contain goodness and overall benefit. Additionally, wisdom is the objective of the believer that wherever he finds it he takes it.*
>
> *However this has a condition, that these matters do not have within them that which opposes the religion or the guidelines of the Sharee'ah. We wish for civilization and we wish for development! One can work to bring this about, but he must be warned against opposing the guidelines and guidance of the Sharee'ah in any matters.*
>
> *We, as Muslims, do not oppose what is called civilization. The one who attempts to describe us with this false description is someone unjust and is a deceiver. How could this be the case when the scholars of the Muslims were those who were the leaders of new discoveries in*

---

[10] Definitive Responses to Doubts and Misconceptions that Have Arisen pg. 2
[11] From the Facebook page of Sheikh Muhammad Baazmool, Ramadhaan 21, 1437

every field of practical knowledge? As such, those who attempt to describe the Muslim or Islaam as reactionary or backwards, then they simply do not understand Islaam, and they're discussing something that they don't properly comprehend. Or it may be the case that they themselves only desire civilization and advancement and development which has been stripped free of the religion of Islaam.

So what is the position of the material progress among the priorities of a Muslim? The issue of material progress in the view and priorities of a Muslim is that it is a tool and means but not the goal or objective, meaning by this that he doesn't work and strive for the sake of achieving it simply for its own sake. Rather he works towards developing the world for the goal of establishing the Sharee'ah of Allaah, and being successfully prepared for the Last Day. Since this worldly life is considered only similar to a tree in which you take shade under briefly while traveling and then you leave it behind!"

He, may Allaah preserve him, also said in addressing some of those Muslims who wrongly have accepted some of these misconceptions,[12]

"Some say, [The Sharee'ah is not suitable to be implemented in our current age.]

We say in response, "The Sharee'ah is suitable and enables the best of benefits and interests in every age and time.

They say, [But the Sharee'ah, must change and be adapted as the times and places change.]

We say in response, "Those specific rulings which are directly connected to restricted issues and variable

[12] From the Facebook page of the Sheikh Muhammad Baazmool

conditions that change such as varying custom, independently derived rulings, and achieving specific greater social benefits, then these do in fact change as the times and places, change."

They say, [I am training some of the children from the next generation to rise up with Islaam in the coming future.]

*We say in response, "Yet, Allaah the Blessed and the Most High, commanded, ◈ **And warn your tribe (O Muhammad) of near kindred.**◈–(Surah ash-Shu'ara': 214) And the Messenger, may the praise and salutations of Allaah be upon him, said what means, "**Start with yourself....then the next closest, and the next closest.**"'*

This very serious misconception, that the Muslims need a new improved version of Islaam which is adjusted and tailored to the current age and or society, not the original revealed religion the first generations made a reality, will never be accurate no matter how many different ways it is put forward or how many times it is repeated. Because as Sheikh Saaleh al-Fauzaan Sheikh, may Allaah preserve him, stated,[13]

"The methodology which is from that of the first three generations of this Ummah is suitable for every age and location on earth, because it is light that has come from Allaah, the Most Glorified and the Most Exalted. So it can never truly be diminished by the words of those detractors."

From those serious challenges facing a new Muslim, especially prominent in our age are those false scholars or pretenders to comprehensive knowledge who the common people are beguiled to wrongly turn to as scholars to guide them in their lives. This danger was foretold to us by the Messenger of Allaah, may the praise and salutations of

[13] The Need of the Ummah for the Salafee Methodology pg. 12

Allaah be upon him, in several authentic narrations. It first occurred in the first centuries of Islaam with the false leaders of the early misguided sects such as the Khawaarij. As Imaam Maalik, may Allaah have mercy upon him, said, [14]

> *"There is never a scarcity of knowledge of the transmitted reports of knowledge among a people, except that among them desires spring forth and are wrongly followed. There is never a scarcity of scholars among a people, except that among them foolish worthless ones then spring forth and are wrongly followed."*

This dangerous situation is also shown in the description of Ibn Battah al-'Ukbaree, may Allaah have mercy upon him, from over a thousand years ago,[15]

> *"The people of our age drift and float just as a bird does following others in a flock. Despite them knowing that the Messenger of Allaah, may Allaah's praise and salutations be upon him, is the last of the prophets, yet if someone appears among them, who falsely claims prophethood, or someone who wrongly claims to have control over aspects of Allaah's creations, then inevitably you will find there is someone to follow him and those people who will align themselves with him as a group."*

This danger is even more frequent in our modern century and has been warned about by the true scholars of our age. The guiding hadeeth scholar Sheikh al-Albaanee, may Allaah have mercy upon him, said in discussing the misguided individual named as-Saqqaf, and those like him, who were false claimants to having firm Sharee'ah knowledge,[16]

[14] Dham al-Kalaam of al-Haraawee, vol. 5 page 79
[15] Al-Ibaanah, al-Kubraa vol.1 page 108 This steadfast scholar from the past scholars who stood upon and called to the Sunnah lived close to a thousand years ago. What would someone with his concern for guidance and insight say about the state of the people today, and the ease with which some easily follow any every false claimant who have devised a path that he or she wishes to call to.
[16] Silsilaat al-Hadeeth as-Saheehah, vol. 2 pg. 713

"And Allaah's assistance is sought from the corruption of the people which is found in this age, where every person is amazed with his own opinion.

By Allaah, the One whom there is none worthy of worship Other than Him, many of the people are deceived and beguiled by any work which is printed and publishing by any individual at all, they believe the shiny mirage of water to be real, and wrongly suppose that what is actually almost empty has some meat of true knowledge. Yet the true state of such people is as was said in the past "A empty bone with only a bit of meat clinging to it…"

How many people have come to wrongly stand before the people of the world as scholars, calling to both old and new forms of misguidance?! The guiding scholar Sheikh Saaleh Ibn Fauzaan, may Allaah preserve him, said,[17]

These efforts of calling to the religion which have been given the label "Islamic" generally do not give importance to establishing the foundation of the correct beliefs of Islaam. They place correct beliefs as something which will come as after their different efforts, not as something which is at the head of and central to the efforts of calling to the religion. It is for this reason that these calls will all ultimately be unsuccessful and eventual failures."

The severe danger in this for the new Muslim is that he or she may not have the knowledge needed to discern the weakness in the claim to authentic knowledge, in what those who claim to have sound knowledge in what they commonly put forth today of videos, tweets, and blog posts. Yet the senior guiding scholars who understand and defend the methodology of the people upon the Sunnah struggle diligently to prevent the general people from being deceived by such people. As an example of this, Sheikh

---

[17] From a lecture 'Lessons From the Sunnah' given 10-11-1437

'Abdul-Muhsin al-'Abbad, may Allaah preserve him, discussing those who influenced Saaleh al-Maghaamsee, who has fallen into different kinds of misguidance that have been clarified, by Sheikh al-'Abbad and other senior scholars such as Sheikh Saaleh al-Fauzaan, may Allaah preserve them both, mentioned,[18]

> "....This is an example of what comes forth from the books of these three misguided sects of those matters of falsehood that they stand upon. Indeed Hasan Ibn Farhan al-Maalaki has made this clear in what is found on the internet of his pleasure with this statement of al-Maghaamsee. He stated [This is what he said to me while in his home about a month ago, and I encouraged him to spread it publicly.] This makes clear that these statements issued by al-Maghaamsee are the result of having evil sitting companions and their negative influence.
>
> Yet this is not something strange to occur from al-Maalaki, as it is clear that his heart has already been seared and burned with hatred and rancor against the Companions of the Messenger of Allaah, as well as towards those Muslims who have followed their path throughout time. I have refuted him scholastically in two separate works. The most recent of which is dated 2/26/1434, and is entitled, "The Rafidhee Deviant Hasan Al-Maalaki Prefers Khomaynee To The Prophet's Scribe Mu'aweeyah, May Allaah Be Pleased With Him, Who Wrote Down Revelation." In fact he, this lying deceiver, has clearly stated that Khomaynee [19] is much better that him meaning Mu'aweeyah! And all of this is documented on the internet.

---

[18]   From the main website of the Sheikh al-'Abbad - article number 299858

[19]   For a more detailed discussion of the error and misguidance of Khomaynee refer to the introduction of Book 1 of the Usul as-Sunnah course

Our our Lord, do not cause our hearts to deviate after you have guided us. Cause us to love those, and grant for us that tremendous mercy coming from you, certainly you are al-Wahhaab the Giver. Our Lord! Forgive us and our brethren who have preceded us in Faith, and put not in our hearts any hatred against those who have believed. Our Lord! You are indeed full of kindness, Most Merciful."

From the inward challenges faced by the new Muslim and the newly committed Muslim is struggling with old ideas, thoughts, feelings, connections, and relationships from before they were blessed to made the courageous and natural choice to follow Allaah's guidance. Sheikh Muhammad Baazmool was asked,[20] **Question: Is love or attraction of someone something considered from falsehood, even if you are not acting upon or connected outwardly to them, meaning that it is only internal? Indeed, we hope and ask Allaah to direct us towards closeness with those whom He loves for us and that they be made to be those permissible for us.**

"Islaam does not blame an individual for those inward thoughts that a person struggles with and keeps control of, meaning that which comes forth without him having any control of them occurring, regardless of this being feelings of love or feelings of hatred. The religion of Islaam teaches and guides a Muslim how to direct those feelings in a legitimate and permissible direction.

*As such, concerning what was mentioned by the questioner, there is no harm in that, as long as a Muslim or Muslimah does not fall into committing what is prohibited in Islaam. It was narrated from Ibn 'Abbaas that the Messenger of Allaah said {**There is nothing like marriage, for two who love one another.**}[21]*

---

[20] As found on the Sheikh's website bazmool.net
[21] Sunan Ibn Maajah no. 1920, and it was authenticated by Imaam al-Albaanee in his work Silsilaat al-Hadeeth as-Saheehah, narration number 624

*The meaning of his statement, may the praise and salutations of Allaah be upon him,: {**There is nothing like marriage, for two who love one another.**} is that legitimate marriage increases the love between a man and woman who love each other. As such Islaam guides the one who falls in love to proceed to get married to the one whom they have love for, if that is feasible. Or guides them to marry another individual, since it does not hold that there is anything better than marriage for those with love for each other.*

Through this, it is seen that Islaam does not deny basic human nature, but only directs it towards that action which contain true good and contentment for it, both in this world and in the Hereafter. Similarly, it is narrated about hatred and dislike that is found in the heart that Abu Hurairah, may Allaah be pleased with him, narrated:

The Messenger of Allaah said, in that related narration, there is the additional statement, (narrated by Imaam Muslim in his Saheeh: narration number 2564). Within this hadeeth narration, there is from the Messenger of Allaah, may the praise and salutations of Allaah be upon him, a prohibition for a Muslim engaging in what will cause him to fall into hatred, discord, and rancor between a Muslim and his brothers. So Islaam guides them to abandon and turn away from that. It explains to them that a Muslim should recognize the right of his Muslim brother, and that it is not permissible for him to trespass against his blood, honor, or wealth. And the success is from Allaah."

There is also little question that one the most significant or difficult challenges for a new Muslim, the issue of friends and companionship. Sheikh al-'Utheimeen, may

Allaah have mercy upon him, said, [22]

"It is necessary that an intelligent person carefully considers who his friends and companions are. Are they people involved in some form of evil or wrongdoing? If so, then he must move away from them as they are a worse enemy and affliction upon him than being infected with the physical disease of skin mange or scabies.

Or are his friends people of goodness? Those who encourage and enjoin on him towards goodness and prevent him from entering into wrongdoing, and open the doors of goodness to various matters for him. If they are like this, then he should stick with them."

Certainly, the benefit of good friends even extends beyond this life. From the scholars of that Salaf that reminded us of their benefit in the next life was al-Hasan al-Basree, may Allaah have mercy upon him, who was reported to have said,[23]

"Seek to have many friends from the believing Muslims, as they will be a source of intercession for you on the Day of Resurrection."

Sheikh al-'Utheimeen, may Allaah have mercy upon him, was also asked, **"Some of the people if they withdraw from mixing with others generally their emaan or faith increases and the desires to achieve good increases, whereas if they mix with them they slip into heedlessness. So which of these two ways is better?"** He responded, [24]

*"We say that if this individual has knowledge by which the general people would be benefited by and would be guided to what is correct by then his choosing to mix with them is given priority, as {**The believer who mixes with the people and is patient upon the harms that he***

---

[22] Qawl al-Mufeed Alaa Kitaab at-Tawheed: vol. 1, 363
[23] Tafseer al-Baghawee, vol. 8 pg. 340
[24] Liqaa' al-Bab Maftuh 14/234

receives from them is better that the Muslim who does not mix with them without being patient upon such harms.}

But as for the case where the individual is just from the common Muslims and he does not mix with the people fearing the negative results of that for himself, yet properly establishing his required acts of worship -then he can do this. However he should not separate away from his family as he is directly responsible for his family. Since, a man has within his care those people who are within his house and is responsible for those under his care."

He, may Allaah have mercy upon him, and grant him the best of rewards, also explained that,[25]

"If the time and age you live in is in many ways corrupt, such that you see and recognize that your mixing often with people does not bring you anything other than harm and is damaging and in fact distances you from Allaah, then you should incline toward being by yourself."

Sheikh al-'Utheimeen, may Allaah have mercy upon him, focusing upon the importance of spreading beneficial knowledge mentioned in his explanation of the work Riyaadh al-Saaliheen,

"The unknown individual: He is the one who does not put himself forward and who is not concerned with being in front of the people or being talked about by the young, or the people discussing him. But you find him someone who goes from his house to the masjid, and then from the masjid back to his house. Then he may go from his house to visit some close relatives or some of his Muslim brothers, but he remains generally unknown.

---

[25] His explanation of Riyaadh as-Saaliheen, vol. 5 pg. 354

However, an individual should not chose this if Allaah has blessed him with knowledge, such that he simply remains in his home and not convey knowledge to the people. This contradicts what should be done by the one who fears Allaah. That he should strive to teach the people goodness and what benefits them is better than him isolating himself in his house without benefiting anyone with his knowledge, or by simply sitting in his house without benefiting any of the people with the wealth he possesses.

Yet, if the matter is between being prominent, standing forth with renown among others, putting himself forward to shine, and between remaining unknown then in this case he should chose to be unknown. But when it becomes required that he be in front of the people, due to his knowledge, then he should stand forth. This should be done by the way of spreading his knowledge among the people, and establishing lessons, and study circles in every possible place. Similarly it is through the means of offering the Friday khutbah on the day of Jumu'ah, the days of 'eid, and other instances. Since undertaking this is something beloved to Allaah, the Most Glorified and the Most Exalted."

From among those challenges is becoming steadfast upon the obligatory prayer, when the focus of society is directed towards the pleasure of self not the pleasure of Allaah. The eminent Sheikh Sheikh 'Abdul-'Azeez Ibn Baaz, may Allaah have mercy upon him, explained the verse [26] **And those who guard their Salaat (prayers) well, Such shall dwell in the Gardens (i.e. Paradise) honored. -(Surah al-Ma'aarij: 34-35).**

"This indicates that the performance of the obligatory ritual prayer is a determining criterion, and that whoever opposes the guidance regarding it and fails to

[26] Explanation of Kitaab at-Tawheed from Saheeh al-Bukhaaree: pg 384

implement it, has turned away and opposed every good generally. Likewise, whoever establishes and preserves the duty of the obligatory prayer will achieve every form and kind of good available."

Indeed the importance of the Muslim man being connected to the masjid nearby is well known among the people and books of righteousness. Ibn Rajab, may Allaah have mercy upon him, said,

"The individual who adheres firmly to the houses of Allaah engaging in worship, he is considered a soldier striving in the path of Allaah, opposing and fighting his own desires. This is from the best forms of having patience and engaging in jihaad."

It is important that we each remember as we struggle daily that Allaah will strengthen our efforts, once we take steps forward and strive for His sake with sincerity and resolve. Al-Haafidh Ibn Rajab, may Allaah have mercy upon him, also said, [27]

"Know that your own self has the position similar to your riding animal. If it knows that you are putting forth effort to move forward, it moves toward doing so a similar way, and if your wish is to be lazy it grasps hold of this, and seeks from you its portion of that and then directs you toward simply fulfilling your desires."

Sheikh al-'Utheimeen, may Allaah have mercy upon him, encourages us by saying, [28]

"Some of the people if they unsuccessfully attempt to accomplish something one or two times, they become pessimistic - feeling that they will never be successful and so give up on it. But doing so is a mistake. Since every matter in which real benefit can be found, you should not simply drop and start to neglect it the first time you

[27] Majmu'a Rasaa'il Ibn Rajab vol. 3 pg. 185
[28] Majmu'a al-Fataawa: vol. 9, pg. 516

are not successful regarding it. Rather try another time until Allaah opens ways for your success."

Al-Haafidh Ibn Jawzee, may Allaah have mercy upon him, points out the contradiction of some of people giving detail and significant concern to worldly affairs, but neglecting the affairs of their religion,[29]

"Oh you, plan and organize the affairs of your religion just as you do so for your worldly affairs. Just as if you found a pin sticking within your clothing, you would stop and go back to remove it before proceeding. Similarly there are sins that like a pin persistently getting stuck within your heart, yet if you accustom yourself to considering and viewing them with dissatisfaction and regret, there are removed from it."

We should also look at those who have failed to both put efforts into their affairs by truly struggling and then relying upon Allaah for final success, and take note of the general affect that this has. Ibn al-Qayyim, may Allaah have mercy upon him, said, [30]

"The people who are lazy are more generally found to be plagued by concerns, worries, and low spirits. They rarely find delight and joy in their condition as opposed to those who are committed to putting forth efforts and working in their affairs."

How true is the statement that Umar Ibn al-Khattab, may Allaah have mercy upon him, is reported to have said, [31]

"The truly weak man is he who is too weak to manage himself."

And he, the second of the rightly guided Khalifahs, may Allaah be pleased with him, is also reported to have said insupplication,[32]

[29] al-Mahadash, page 116
[30] Rawdah al-Muhibeen. vol. 1 pg. 168
[31] Adab ad-Dunya wa ad-Deen of al-Mawroode, pg. 18
[32] Musannaf Ibn Abee Shaybah, no. 5179

"O Allaah, I am weak, so strengthen me. I am harsh, so make me gentle. I am miserly, so make me generous."

So it is important to know that you are responsible for working towards your own good, and establishing a life based upon the fear of Allaah and His obedience, in order to be successful in this world and the next. Sheikh Muhammad Baazmool, mentioned that,

"Every Muslim is responsible, because every Muslim must have taqwa or the fear of Allaah. Allaah, the Most Perfect and the Most High, said, ❀ **No doubt! Verily, the close associates of Allaah [i.e. those who believe in the Oneness of Allaah and fear Allaah much (abstain from all kinds of sins and evil deeds which he has forbidden), and love Allaah much (perform all kinds of good deeds which He has ordained)], no fear shall come upon them nor shall they grieve. Those who believed (in the Oneness of Allaah - Islamic Monotheism), and used to fear Allaah much (by abstaining from evil deeds and sins and by doing righteous deeds). For them are glad tidings, in the life of the present world (i.e. righteous dream seen by the person himself or shown to others), and in the Hereafter. No change can there be in the Words of Allaah, this is indeed the supreme success.** ❀*-(Surah Yunus: 62-64).*

Further clarifying this, the basis and foundation of taqwa is placing between you and between the punishment of Allaah a barrier, but fulfilling His commands and staying away from what He has prohibited. This general description is one which every single Muslim is included within. Taqwa or the fear of Allaah has several levels:

The first level: the obligatory fearing of Allaah. The intended meaning of this level is that it is required upon every mature capable Muslim to fulfill and establish those matters which are obligatory upon him in the Sharee'ah and remain away from those matters prohibited from

him by the Sharee'ah.

The second level, is the recommended fearing of Allaah. This is an increase upon what is established from the first level by also undertaking those recommended actions which are not at the level of being obligatory as well as staying away from disliked matters that are not at the level of being forbidden.

The third level: the completion or perfection of fearing Allaah. It is a higher level than the previous two, in that a Muslim, in addition to what is established on the first two levels, he avoids those neutral matters available to him out of piety and righteousness.

Additionally, it is possible that a Muslim may fall short in some of the matters required from having the obligatory fear of Allaah, such that his taqwa has a deficiency. Yet overall he's still considered among those who fear Allaah generally. The people of Islaam vary in their degree, upon many different levels of having this important characteristic, in fact differ in every single level of fearing Allaah. Allaah we ask you to raise up our degrees and levels of having taqwa as certainly our flesh and bodies may not fear the Fire. Allaah make us of those who are guided and who guide others not from those who are astray and who send others astray."

Imaam adh-Dhahabee, may Allaah have mercy upon him, points out the importance of properly judging our success according to how and where we ultimately end up. He mentioned, speaking historically about an individual named Hallaaj,[33]

"He had a good beginning, but they he began to stray and veered towards the misguidance of Sufism, eventually he abandoned the religion of Islaam all together. Indeed,

---

[33] Mizaan al-'Itidaal vol. 1 pg. 548

what is considered is the end or conclusion of one's life not simply how one started out. Oh Allaah we seek steadfastness from you."

The scholars of the tawheed, those who focus on properly establishing the worship of Allaah alone, have always taught the importance of seeking Allaah's assistance in working to remain steadfast upon the guidance of the Prophet, may the praise and salutations of Allaah be upon him. How important such supplication should be to us in our current age and condition![34] Ibn Shaaheen, in his work Sharh Madhaahib Ahlus-Sunnah, said,[35]

"From those supplication comes from those who came before us is, "O Allaah, show me the truth to be recognized as being the truth and enable me to follow it. And show me falsehood to be recognized as being falsehood and enable me to turn away from it."

---

[34] It is permissible for a Muslim to supplicate to Allaah alone in any language he understands as is mentioned by the reliable scholars upon the Sunnah. In response to the question, *"Is it permissible to supplicate in the English language?"* The Permanent Committee for Scholarly Research and Ifta' replied: "It is permissible for an individual to supplicate to Allaah,the Most Exalted, the Most Magnificent, in any language which a person understands, whether that is the Arabic language, English, Urdu, or another language. And the success is from Allaah. May the praise and salutations of Allaah be upon our Prophet Muhammad, his household , and his Companions." - third question from ruling no. 6348 vol. 3 , pg. 388- from the collected rulings of the Permanent Committee for Scholarly Research and Ifta'

[35] Sharh Madhaahib Ahlus-Sunnah: pg. 40

Some of the challenges facing a new Muslim or a Muslim who is newly committed to learning and living Islaam properly, are directly related to changing and developing the proper perspectives and way of looking at our life as a whole. The correct view of life is something which the sound aqeedah or beliefs of Islaam cultivate with the Muslims, and it is reflected in what they give importance to. For this reasons when we fail to understand the nature of life properly it affects everything else we do and turn towards. When the noble Companion Suhaib, may Allaah be pleased with him, one of the early Muslim living in Mecca attempted to migrate to Medinah, the disbelieving Quraish said to him,

> *"You came to us as a destitute beggar and have grown rich among us, and now you want to go away safely with your life and wealth. By God, it shall never be so!"*
>
> *Suhayb asked,* "Would you allow me to go if I give my property to you?"
>
> *When they replied in the affirmative, Suhayb said,* "Then I will give you all of it."
>
> *After his successful emigration to Medinah, when the Prophet, may the praise and salutations of Allaah be upon him, was told about the incident, he exclaimed,* {**Suhaib has made a profit! Suhaib has made a profit!**} [36]

His courage and willingness to sacrifice for Islaam, may Allaah be pleased with him, shows us the importance of reminding ourselves and others of the true value of our beliefs and religion compared to the nature of our passing life and time here on earth. We must reexamine what we consider a good life, and what it takes to have one. Sheikh

[36] As transmitted in Ibn Katheer, vol.2, pg.233

al-'Utheimeen, may Allaah have mercy upon him, was asked,[37] *"What is the meaning of that good life where Allaah says, ◈ Whoever works righteousness, whether male or female, while he (or she) is a true believer (of Islamic Monotheism) verily, to him We will give a good life (in this world with respect, contentment and lawful provision), and We shall pay them certainly a reward in proportion to the best of what they used to do ◈-(Surah an-Nahl: 97)*. He answered, may Allaah have abundant mercy upon him,

"A good life is that in which one's heart generally finds a state of ease and pleasure and they are blessed with peace of mind and serenity. Such that even when individual finds himself in a state of distress and hardship, his heart is at peace and his mind is untroubled. The Prophet, may Allaah's praise and salutations be upon him, stated, {How wonderful is the case of a believer; there is good for him in everything and this applies only to a believer. If prosperity attends him, he expresses gratitude to Allaah and that is good for him; and if adversity befalls him, he endures it patiently and that is better for him}.[38]

But in comparison, the disbeliever if he is tested with a calamity does he usually proceed with the needed patience? The answer is no, he may become depressed and it seems like the entire world it closing in upon him, to the degree that perhaps he may even decide to kill himself and so commits suicide. Yet the believer is patient and experiences the inner comfort of having that patience. Some of the scholars of history have remarked upon this regarding an incident in the life of Ibn Hajr al-Asqalaanee, may Allaah have mercy upon him. In his age he was appointed as a judge in the land of Egypt.

---

[37] Aadab Taalib al-Ilm, Book of Knowledge by Sheikh al-'Utheimeen: 36-37
[38] Narrated by Muslim: 2999, ad-Darimee in his Sunan: 2777 and the Musnad of Imaam Ahmad: vol.4 pg.332

*It was related that when he came to the neighborhood where he was working you would see many carts and wagons pulled by horses or mules transporting goods. One day upon arrival in that neighborhood there was a Egyptian Jewish man who would sell oil. As was common he, like that those transporting oil, would have his clothes stained by the oil in the containers. This Jewish man who was a common laborer, stopped his cart, and came up to Ibn Hajr.. He said to Ibn Hajr, may Allaah have mercy upon him, [Your prophet said that { **The world is a prison for the believing Muslims and a paradise for the disbelievers.**} Yet look, you are someone who is a judge among from the prominent judges of Egypt. You live in contentment and proceed in a life of ease. Whereas look at me, (meaning by this that this Jewish man was in a state of difficulty, due to his work and station in life)!]*

Ibn Hajr said, "As for me, regarding my current state of comfort and ease, when it is accurately compared in relation to the pleasures available in Paradise, it is as harsh and difficult as a prison. And as for you then the difficulty and hardship you currently find yourself in, it is like as a paradise in comparison to the punishment awaiting you in Hellfire because of your disbelief. Upon hearing this the Jewish man said, "I bear witness that there is none worthy of worship except Allaah, and I bear witness that Muhammad is the messenger of Allaah", and he entered into Islaam.

So we must understand that the believer is in a state of goodness regardless of what situation he finds himself in. Whatever it is, it contains true profit for him in this world as well as the Hereafter. While a disbeliever is in a state of loss regardless of what situation he finds himself in, since even if unrecognized he actually losing both the best of this world and that of the Hereafter, due to his disbelief. Allaah, the Most High, says, ❖By Al-'Asr (the time) Verily! Man is in loss, Except those who believe (in Islamic Monotheism) and do righteous good deeds, and recommend one another to the truth (i.e. order one another to perform all kinds of good deeds (Al-Ma'roof) which Allaah has ordained, and abstain from all kinds of sins and evil deeds (Al-Munkar)which Allaah has forbidden), and recommend one another to patience (for the sufferings, harms, and injuries which one may encounter in Allaah's Cause during preaching His religion of Islamic Monotheism or Jihaad, etc.❖

Anas bin Maalik, may Allaah be pleased with him, narrated that the Messenger of Allaah, may the praise and salutations of Allaah be upon him, said, [39]

{Whoever makes the Hereafter his goal, Allaah makes his heart rich, and organizes his affairs, and the world comes to him whether it wants to or not.

And whoever makes the world his goal, Allaah puts his poverty right before his eyes, and disorganizes his affairs, and the world does not come towards him, except what has been decreed for him.}

Al-Hasan al-Basree, may Allaah have mercy upon him, clarifies that this is a unique perspective,[40]

" The believer is like a stranger in this worldly life, he does not become overly concerned with what it offers nor does he compete in seeking its temporary glories. The people of focus on this world have their concern, and the believer has his own different distinct concern."

Sheikh al-'Utheimeen, may Allaah, the Most High, have mercy upon him, also clarified some of the misconceptions that those who lack a foundation of the sound beliefs of

---

[39] Jamee'a at-Tirmidhee: 2653 -authenticated by Sheikh al-Albaanee in Silsilat al-Hadeeth as-Saheehah #949, due to several supporting narrations which strengthen this one.
[40] As narrated in Jamee' Ulum al-Hikam of Ibn Hajab al-Hanbalee

Islaam, often hold. He mentioned that,[41]

"Having a good life is not, as some people understand it, never encountering disease, poverty, sickness, or such difficulties. No, rather having a good life means that a person has a good sound heart, whose inward feelings are at ease and comfortable with whatever is from the decree of Allaah and whatever Allaah has preordained for them.

Such that if Allaah has decreed for him well-being and prosperity, he responds with thankfulness, as this response is what is good for him. And if Allaah has decreed that he face hardships and difficulties, then he reacts with patience, and this is response is itself what is good for him.

This is a description of the truly good life, and what brings peace of mind and tranquility of one's heart. As for merely having abundant wealth, and health of one's physical body, then these two could in fact could be a reason or lead to someone being unhappiness and in misery, and they at times might only lead to having more hardships and difficulties."

He also, may Allaah have mercy upon him, reminded us that, [42]

"Every person, as long as his soul is still within his body, is someone who will encounter trials. For this reason I advise myself, and all of you, that we constantly ask Allaah for steadfastness in our emaan or faith, and that we be concerned and worried about this. Since beneath your feet are the slippery tracks of life, and if Allaah, the Most Glorified and the Most Exalted, does not make you steady and steadfast, you may slip into ruin and disaster.

---

[41] Islamic Rulings: vol. 3, pg. 64
[42] as-Sharh al-Mumta' vol. 5 pg. 388

Listen all of you, to the statements of Allaah, the Most Perfect and the Most High directed to His 'Messenger, may Allaah's praise and salutations be upon him, who was unquestioningly the most steadfast of creation and the strongest of them in his emaan or faith, where Allaah said to him, **And had We not made you stand firm, you would nearly have inclined to them a little.** *-(Surah al-Isra': 74). Meaning you would have inclined, if he would have done so, toward them to a small degree.*

So if this was said to the Messenger of Allaah, may Allaah's praise and salutations be upon him, so then what about us? We, as an Ummah, are weak in our faith and in our inward certainty of the truth, and we have been afflicted by both misconceptions and many desires that are followed. We stand in a position of tremendous danger, and it is upon us to ask Allaah, the Most High, to bless us with steadfastness upon the truth, and to not allow or send our hearts astray. This is from the most essential supplications, **Our Lord! Let not our hearts deviate (from the truth) after You have guided us...** *-(Surah Aal-Imraan: 8)*

Sheikh Muhammad Baazmool, explaining this distinct vision of life which the sound beliefs and methodology of Islaam develops within knowledgeable Muslims, said,[43]

"There is a fundamental understanding that I always strive in establishing, and with which I begin with you by mentioning it. On the authority of Abee 'Awn, who said, "The people of goodness if they meet one another they would advise each other with the following:

'The one who works for his success in the next life Allaah suffices him for his success in this world.

And the one who rectifies the relationship between him

---

[43] As narrated on his Facebook page on April 28, 2016

and Allaah, Allaah suffices him for his relationships with the people.

And the one who rectified his inner self, Allaah rectifies for him who he is outwardly.' (al-Musannaf of Ibn Abee Shaybah vol. 7, page 162)"

Reminding us that the true scales are those of Allaah, and to not simply judge according to how those around us judge, Sheikh al-'Utheimeen, may Allaah have mercy upon him, said,[44]

"A man may have achieved the highest position available in the world, yet he may have no worth or value at all with Allaah. Likewise, someone in their place in the world may be lowly, and not regarded as important or significant by the people, yet in the sight of Allaah he is considered as someone better than many other men considered and put together.

We ask Allaah, the Most High to make us and you of those who have true distinction and prominence with Him, and the He places us and you along with those who have a high and eminent position in His estimation: the prophets, the truthful ones, the martyrs, and the righteous people."

Ibn al-Qayyim, may Allaah have mercy upon him, states that being guided to see things in the proper way and according to the right criterion is itself a foundational blessing for a Muslim,[45]

"The one who does not recognize the blessings of Allaah upon him except in the food and drink he's been given and the general health of his body, is not someone who has even the least amount of intelligence. Since the blessing of Allaah within Islaam and faith, and Him inspiring His worshipers towards devotion and

[44] His explanation of Riyaadh as-Saaliheen, vol. 3 pg. 53
[45] Madaarij as-Saalikeen vol.1 pg. 277

*embarking upon this, and coming to take pleasure in
his obedience, is clearly the greatest blessing possible. It is
through recognizing this, that some can affirm that their
intellect has been characterized by having light within
it, and know that someone has been given guidance and
been directed towards true success."*

There is little doubt that some of the problems, leading
to our general weakness, which are prevalent among the
Muslims in this century, are connected directly to the
focus upon worldly wealth and what is connected to its
pursuit for the sake of that wealth itself, not as a means
to please Allaah. The difference between viewing worldly
success and wealth as a means and not just an end is very
important and something Sheikh al-'Utheimeen, may
Allaah have mercy upon him, points out,[46]

> *"You will find that the people who are connected and
> focused upon success in the Hereafter do not give great
> concern to what passes them by of worldly things. When
> something of the benefits of the world reaches them. they
> accept it, but if it passes them by, it is not something
> given true importance by them."*

He, may Allaah have mercy upon him, also warned us, as
our Messenger warned us,[47]

> *"People generally, whenever they increase in the luxury
> and affluence, and this condition of indulgence spreads
> among the people, then different forms of harm and
> evil begin to spread among them also. As this unneeded
> luxury is something leading to a person's weakening and
> then ruin. Since whenever someone looks at what a life
> of luxury offers them, and focuses upon obtaining ease
> in his physical wants, he becomes heedless in striving to
> obtain what his heart truly needs.*

---

[46] His explanation of Riyaadh as-Saaliheen, vol. 3 pg. 48
[47] His Explanation of Riyaadh as-Saaliheen, vol. 2 pg. 37

The most important focus he adopts, becomes making his body comfortable and indulging in its pleasures, despite the reality that it, his body, is always steadily moving closer to death and closer to becoming that which will stink and will be eaten by worms! Yet this specific calamity, this false focus, is what is in fact harming the people in this age, the affliction of concentrating on gaining wealth and indulging in pleasures.

It is almost as if you cannot find anyone who is not saying, "What about our house? What about our car? What about our furniture, What about our good food" Even to the degree that you find that some of those individuals studying Sharee'ah knowledge, are unfortunately pursuing that simply for the sake of obtaining a good social standing, such that they can use this as a means to obtain the good pleasures of this world. But humanity has been created to fulfill such an essential and important matter! The world and its bounties are only a means to achieve that. We ask Allaah to make us of those, who use it properly as the means it is towards achieving that greater objective.

Sheikh al-Islaam Ibn Taymeeyah, may Allaah have mercy upon him, said, 'It is necessary and proper that a person uses wealth the way someone uses a donkey for riding, or how someone uses the bathroom only for the purpose of relieving themselves.' Look at how they, the righteous Muslims, properly understood the place and purpose of worldly wealth, how they understood it limits. So do not make wealth your central focus in life! You should ride wealth toward good, but do not allow the pursuit of wealth to ride you, drive you, and carry you away, such that your most important pursuit becomes passing material success in the world.

It is for this reason it is said that when the opportunity for gaining the material wealth of the world is opened for them, people, they often turn and focus on fully pursuing it, while at the same time they begin to weaken and slip in their efforts for gaining success in the Hereafter, according to the degree that they have turned and began to be carried away by the focus of seeking material successes in this world.

*The Prophet, may Allaah's praise and salutations be upon him, said, {**By Allaah, it is not poverty that I fear for you, but I fear that this world will be opened up with its wealth for you as it was opened to those before you; and you compete with one another over it as they did and eventually it will ruin you as it eventually ruined them**}. (Saheeh Muslim: 457) Indeed the Messenger of Allaah, may Allaah's praise and salutations be upon him, spoke truthfully.*

This is something which is clearly ruining the people today! This matter of competing for worldly success and making its pursuit as if it was the purpose for which they were created is devastating people today. Rather the world was created for them, not them for it. Yet they have become preoccupied and focused upon something created for them as a means, instead of occupied with the essential purpose of worship for which they were created. This is a turning of affairs backwards from how they should be, so we ask Allaah to grant us health and well-being."

Sheikh Hamaad Ibn Muhammad al-Ansaaree, may Allaah have mercy upon him, said many years ago,[48]

"This age that we find ourselves within, I have called it the world of the sleeping or the age of dozing, and the reason for this is the fact that people now have a deep focus on luxury and seeking pleasures."

[48]   al-Majmu'a from the Biography of Sheikh Hamaad Ibn Muhammad al-Ansaaree pg. 587

We should ask ourselves what he would say now seeing the level people's current preoccupation with wealth and worldly pursuits as goals in and of themselves. Sheikh Muqbil Ibn Haadee Al-Waadi'ee, may Allaah have mercy upon him, reminds us that we should not compromise for the sake of worldly advancement,[49]

> *"Know, may Allaah grant you and us success, than being poor upon honor, is better that being wealthy upon disgrace."*

This focus and perspective is what the first generations of Islaam, may Allaah have mercy upon them all, both practiced and taught to others. As is seen when a man came to Wahb Ibn Manabah and said, **"Teach me something by which Allaah will benefit me."** He replied, [50]

> *"Frequently remember that death is coming, and restrict those hopes that you have for this life."*

This is also reflected in the statement of Ibn Taymeeyah, may Allaah have mercy upon him, who said,[51]

> *"That worldly hardship and difficulty that you acknowledge and accept upon faith in Allaah, is better for you than that worldly blessing that leads you towards being forgetful of the remembrance of Allaah."*

What is very important to emphasize is that building one's life upon this correct perspective is only accomplished through seeking authentic Sharee'ah knowledge upon sincerity. Sheikh Saaleh al-Fauzaan, may Allaah preserve him, said, [52]

> *"The one who wants to make himself successful, who seeks to have his endeavors and deeds accepted, and who wants to be a true Muslim, then it is upon him to give attention to learning the correct beliefs of Islaam. As if*

[49] al-Suyoof al-Baatirah: pg. 261
[50] al-Bidaayah wa al-Nihaayeh, vol. 9, pg. 313
[51] Tasleyat Ahl-Masaa'ib of Manbajee pg. 226
[52] A Selection of Islamic Rulings, vol. 1 pg. 2

he comes to understand the authentic beliefs of Islaam and what conflicts and contradicts then, and what negates and diminishes them, then he is able to build his life endeavors upon this understanding. Yet this will not be accomplished except that he learns from the scholars, those people of sound knowledge and insight who themselves took it from the knowledge taken from the first generations of this Muslim Ummah."

THE IMPORTANCE OF AUTHENTIC KNOWLEDGE

The noble scholars of our age, stand as the inheritors of the Messenger of Allaah, may the praise and salutations of Allaah be upon him, just as the steadfast scholars upon the Sunnah in previous centuries did. They remind us of the tremendous responsibility that each of us, as a Muslim, has towards cultivating our emaan and slowly working toward getting stronger as a worshipper of Allaah daily, and committing ourselves to what that requires without letting worldly concerns distract us. Sheikh Muqbil Ibn Haadee al-Waadi'ee, may Allaah have mercy upon him, also said,[53]

"That which I advise myself with and everyone is that they focus and occupy themselves with gaining Sharee'ah knowledge, as the worries and concerns about worldly affairs never end approaching and reaching you. So be warned against becoming preoccupied by the problems of life. As if we become preoccupied with them, then we will not be able to truly seek knowledge."

Yet Sheikh Muqbil, may Allaah have mercy upon him, offers important encouragement saying,[54]

"From the different hardships you encounter during your efforts to gain knowledge, know that the hunger will eventually go away, and the weariness will in time leave

[53] Al-Bashaa'ir Fe as-Samaa'a al-Mubashir by 'Abdullah Ibn Ayyash al-Ahdal: pg 21
[54] Al-Bashaa'ir Fe as-Samaa'a al-Mubashir by 'Abdullah Ibn Ayyash al-Ahdal: pg 28

*you, as will your being unsteady, but the knowledge you
gain will remain."*

He, may Allaah have mercy upon him, said about realizing
guidance in our lives,[55]

*"After acknowledging that "Knowledge and faith have
an important place." Then we hold, as Mu'adh Ibn Jabal
said, what is left other than us working and struggling
upon both of these two matters."*

We have many incredible examples of the dedication
towards gaining Sharee'ah knowledge found among the
first generations as well as from those who followed in
their clear footsteps. It is narrated on the authority of
Dawood Ibn Rasheed that,[56]

*"Yahyaa Ibn Ma'een inherited from his father a million
dirhams, as well as another fifty thousand dirhams. He
spent all of that in pursuit of the knowledge of hadeeth
such that nothing remained with him, not even shoes to
wear."*

The guiding scholar Sheikh 'Abdul-Muhsin al-'Abaad,
may Allaah preserve him, said,[57]

*"The best way in which one might spend his life, and
utilize his time, is being occupied with knowledge of
the Book of Allaah, the Most Glorified and the Most
Exalted, and the Sunnah of His Messenger, may the
praise and salutations of Allaah be upon him, learning
it as well as teaching it. Within this endeavor, when
placed alongside other beneficial actions and deeds, one
gains success and triumph in both this worldly life and
the next."*

But it is important to recognize and initially be aware
from the beginning that not everyone is successful in this.

[55] Al-Bashaa'ir Fe as-Samaa'a al-Mubashir by 'Abdullah Ibn Ayyash al-Ahdal: pg 21
[56] Sharh Ilal at-Tirmidhee: of Ibn Rajab 1/219
[57] Shatharaat Fee Talabal-'Ilm (4)

As Ibn Badran, may Allaah have mercy upon him, one of the well known scholars of Hanbalee fiqh in his time stated,[58]

"Know that many of the people spent several long years studying knowledge, rather studying even just a single branch of knowledge, without gaining significant results. Perhaps they might spend their entire life struggling in it, yet they never surpass the initial level of one beginning in study.

This is the result of one of two matters: either lacking the natural intellectual abilities needed, and so not having the ability to understand its essential principles and concepts. As for this first cause there is no need to speak about it, nor talk about any wrongly-supposed remedy for it.

Yet the second cause is being ignorant of the correct paths and methods that should be proceeded upon when studying and learning...."

al-Haafidh Imaam adh-Dhahabee, may Allaah have mercy upon him, directs us towards some the central sources of revealed transmitted knowledge and warns about some of the false paths which some wrongly take, which every sincere new Muslim should be aware of,[59]

"It is upon you, all my Muslim brothers, to contemplate the book of Allaah, and then be almost obsessed with taking from the two Saheeh collections of Imaam al-Bukhaaree and Imaam Muslim, then Sunan an-Nisaa'ee, and Riyaadh as-Saaliheen of Imaam an-Nawaawee, as well as his work al-Adhkaar, then you will be successful and have truly succeeded.

---

[58]   al-Madhkal ilaa Madhab al-Imaam Ahmad, vol. 1, pg. 265
[59]   Siyaar 'Alaam an-Nubalaa', vol.19 .pg. 340

But be warned against the speculations and opinions of those who were slaves to various philosophies, and intellectual concepts. As well as from those whose work is only preoccupation in sports and athletics. And be warned against the way of self deprivation adopted by the ascetics, as well as from the worthless speeches from those individuals leading others towards worthless paths.

Since every form of goodness is found in following and adhering to the simple pure religion of Ibraheem. Therefore take your assistance and help from Allaah in this way. Oh Allaah we ask you to guide us to your straight path."

When we consider what we know and the extent of our understanding of different aspects of the merciful religion of Islaam, we realize that we each have varying levels of understanding in different aspects of correct beliefs and righteous deeds, as well as of what opposes both of these. Sheikh 'Abdullah 'Abdur-Raheem al-Bukhaaree, may Allaah preserve him, explains some important distinctions between the people and their understanding the truth or falsehood, and the general or detailed nature of both of these important aspects of understanding,

"There are four categories or types of people in relation to understanding the truth and falsehood

The second matter my brothers, may Allaah grant success to you and to us all, is that seeking knowledge is a difficult path, which requires as has been mentioned, efforts and significant work along with patience, and along with these sincerity for Allaah the Most Exalted, the Most Magnificent, sake alone. The tools of the individual seeking knowledge of the Prophets' hadeeth narrations are as was mentioned by Imaam Yahya Ibn Ma'een in al-Jaamea' by Khateeb al-Baghdadee with an authentic chain of narration, where he said,'The tools of the one seeking to learn the hadeeth narrations of the Prophet are the sincerity, staying away from the major sins, distancing yourself from innovations in the religion, trustworthiness, and coming to be known for being committed to seeking knowledge."

This brings forth what indicates, may Allaah bless you, that in regard to learning Sharee'ah knowledge there are four types of individual in relation to understanding the truth and falsehood. As Allaah the Most Exalted, the Most Magnificent, said, ﴾ **And whoever contradicts and opposes the Messenger (Muhammad) after the right path has been shown clearly to him, and follows other than the believers' way. We shall keep him in the path he has chosen, and burn him in Hell - what an evil destination.** ﴿ *-(Surah an-Nisaa': 115) And Allaah the Most Exalted, the Most Magnificent, said in His Book,* ﴾ **And thus do We explain the ayaat (proofs, evidences, verses, lessons, signs, revelations, etc.) in detail, that the way of the Mujrimoon (criminals, polytheists, sinners), may become manifest.** ﴿ *-(Surah al-An'am: 55). So Allaah the Most Exalted, in His High Magnificence, clearly explained* ﴾**the believers' way.**﴿ *in His Book, specifically, and also clearly explained "the wrongdoers or sinners way." in His Book, specifically, distinguishing between this way and that way. Similarly, the Sunnah comes forward and clearly distinguishes between the first way and the separate second way. Those who possess clear knowledge of Allaah and about His Book, they are the ones who gain that through acquiring detailed knowledge, by specifics about the truth, and specific about falsehood.*

The first of such people were the Companions of the Messenger of Allaah may the praise and salutations of Allaah be upon him and his family. There are those whom Ibn al-Qayyim described, when he discussed these four types of individual, saying, 'They are signposts of guidance'. So the people are of four types:

The first type: those who understand the truth in its specific details, and falsehood in its specific details. These people are those who proceed in the way of the Book of Allaah and the Sunnah, and take hold of whatever is indicated within the two revealed source texts, and adhere firmly to the believers way of the Companions. About these individuals Ibn al-Qayyim mentioned about them, that they were "The most knowledgeable of creation". Indeed, those are truly the most knowledgeable of creation, it is not permissible to have enmity towards them nor go beyond the proper bounds with them, since they are the most knowledgeable of Allaah's creation and since they are signposts of guidance.

He said the second type: 'those who understand the truth in its specific details, and falsehood only generally.' They understand they truth but what opposes it, what about that? The understand that it is falsehood only in a general way. But not the details about that falsehood, and the paths and methods utilized by the people of falsehood, and ways the people of falsehood have of influencing and entering into people affairs. Therefore for such matters like the schemes and plans of the people of falsehood, this type of person does not comprehend and understand them specifically. For this reason generally, that some do not recognize the specific ways of their spreading falsehood, when someone of evil intent enters the ranks of the people the Sunnah, when such an person comes to stand among them the harm they may cause to the people of the Sunnah is significant.

Yes, it is true that the beginning seeker of knowledge is not requested from him that he understand falsehood in all its specific details when he is just beginning his studies. What is obligatory upon him is that he strives to understand the truth and its specifics and that he comes to understand what generally opposes that truth from falsehood. Thereafter when he progresses further and continues to acquire knowledge then he learns the specifics about the truth, along with a portion of the specifics of that falsehood which opposes it. In this way he will eventually come to understand the truth specifically and various aspects of falsehood specifically.

The third type: the one who is hasty. This is the one who only understands the truth only generally and but comprehends the various specific aspects of falsehood. This category of people, they can cause severe harm.

The fourth type, are those who understand the truth only generally and comprehend falsehood only generally. They do not stand in conformity, from either direction, with what was mentioned about the first category, meaning those who understand the truth specifically in its details, and also comprehend aspects of falsehood in a detailed way."

Sheikh Muhammad Ibn Saaleh al-'Utheimeen, may Allaah the Most High, have mercy upon him, said, [60]

"...If a person truly considers and questions: 'What is the purpose for which I was created?' So that he comes to have clear knowledge that he was created for the purpose of worshipping Allaah. Additionally, he was likewise created to eventually live in the coming life of the Hereafter, not in this temporary life. Since this world is a only passage way which is permissible to take from as he travels to the life of the Hereafter as that is the life which he was actually created for, and which it is obligatory that he work towards reaching success in it.

---

[60] Qawl al-Mufeed Alaa Kitaab at-Tawheed: vol. 1, 155

If we only knew, which day from among his days is the last, each person would seriously consider what deeds he has actually put forth?! Such that he should ask himself "How much time do I have left in this life? What have a profited and benefited so far?" Saying to himself, "So many days have passed, yet I am not sure if after them I have increased in closeness to Allaah or fallen into moving further away from him." Have we properly called ourselves to account and considered this subject suitably? As it is only suitable that every intelligent person have a sound objective and goal. But what should that goal be?

We, at present are seeking Sharee'ah knowledge in order to gain closeness to Allaah through seeking of that knowledge, in order to first inform ourselves and also be able to communicate it to others. Yet after we have learned and understood such and such issue- have we also properly implemented it? The reality is that in any situation, we undoubtedly find within ourselves many shortcomings and deficiencies.

Furthermore, as mentioned, after we have come to have knowledge of a matter or issue, have we then also undertaken calling other created servants to it? This is also an issue which requires that we question and call ourselves to account in relation to it.

For that reason, there is no question that the responsibility held by the seeker of knowledge is not an easy one. He is required to pay a significant amount of "zakaat" upon the wealth of possessed knowledge. He is required to implement it and act upon it, and spread his knowledge, and strive to bring about the awareness and comprehension of Islaam among the Ummah of Islaam, otherwise he may end up straying and deviating from the Sharee'ah of Allaah."

Ibn al-Qayyim, may Allaah have mercy upon him said, [61]

> *"The person adhering to the Sunnah, has a heart which
> is alive and which possesses light. Whereas the person
> knowingly involved in innovation in the religion, has
> a heart that is dying and characterized by darkness.
> Allaah, how free from any imperfection is He, has
> mentioned these two clear fundamental realities in His
> Book in more than one place. Furthermore, He made
> the first two characteristics, possessing a heart which is
> alive and has the light of faith, a characteristic of the
> people of emaan or faith. Just as He has indicated that
> the opposite of both of them is a characteristic of those
> who are separated away and outside of faith."*

The guiding scholar Sheikh Saaleh Ibn Fauzaan, may
Allaah preserve him, indicated how this is reflected in our
closeness or distance from our Most Merciful Lord,[62]

> *"Innovations in the religion do not contain any goodness
> whatsoever, but in fact only take you further away from
> Allaah, and earn Allaah, the Most Glorified and the
> Most Exalted's, anger. Whereas the authentic practices of
> the Sunnah contain every aspect of goodness, and cause
> Allaah's pleasure and are what He in fact loves."*

He, may Allaah preserve him, also pointed out the result
of the refusal to adhere only to the Sunnah and the way
of the supporting sunnahs of the guided Khaleefahs, the
Salaf followed,[63]

> *"If individual does not follow and adhere to the guidance
> that the Messenger of Allaah, may Allaah's praise and
> salutations be upon him, proceeded upon, and the*

[61] Ijtima'a al-Jawayesh al-Islameeyah, pg. 39
[62] Explanation of of the Structured Poem al-Ha'eeyah: pg. 53
[63] Explanation of the Advice and Counsel of the Prophet: pg. 13

supporting sunnahs of his rightly guided Khaleefahs, then he will find himself drowning within these trials and tribulations."

He, may Allaah preserve him, also said of those rejecting the way of the first Muslims,[64]

"As for that evidence which is from a sunnah from the established sunnahs of the four rightly guided Khaleefahs, no one rejects them -except someone who is ignorant or a pretender to knowledge."

Sheikh al-'Utheimeen, may Allaah, the Most High, have mercy upon him, within his response to a question asking for a statement that which would make the people of innovation clearly understand the danger of their misguidance and guide them towards what is correct, said,[65]

"...My advice to these individuals involved within these mentioned groups who have left the boundaries of the authentic guidance of the Messenger, due to the innovation they choose to proceed upon, my advice is that they repent to Allaah, the Most Glorified and the Most Exalted, and return back to the guidance of the Book of Allaah, and the Sunnah of His Messenger, may the praise and salutations of Allaah be upon him, which explains and clarifies the Qur'aan. This is, in order that they actually come back to his true guidance, may the salutation and praise of Allaah be upon him, which is a complete implementation of the perfect Sharee'ah of Allaah, and that they come back to the guidance and way of the Companions, at the head of which are the rightly guided Khaleefahs: Abu Bakr, 'Umar' 'Uthmaan, and 'Alee, may Allaah be pleased with all of them.

[64] 'Brief Comments upon the work 'The Yearned For Relief From the Deadly Traps of Shaytaan' From the lecture given on 1-29-1438
[65] Majmua al-Fatawaa wa rasia'l Fadheelatul-Sheikh Muhammad Ibn Saaleh al-'Utheimeen: vol. 27 pg. 436-437

As for these new paths, and these innovations which oppose the true religion of Allaah, they are all actually misguidance regardless of how pleased someone is with them, or how content the hearts of men have become with them, no matter how attractive and appealing they have been made. They remain in essence evil endeavors despite having been made appealing to the people. Just as Allaah the Most High says, ❖ **Is he, then, to whom the evil of his deeds is made fair-seeming, so that he considers it as good (equal to one who is rightly guided)? Verily, Allaah sends astray whom He wills, and guides whom He wills. So destroy not yourself (O Muhammad) in sorrow for them. Truly, Allaah is All-Knower of what they do!** ❖*-(Surah al-Faatir: 8)*

Moreover, one must understand that people can wrongly make their hearts receptive to even accepting disbelief, as Allaah the Most High says, ❖ **Whoever disbelieved in Allaah after his belief, except him who is forced thereto and whose heart is at rest with Faith; but such as open their breasts to disbelief, on them is wrath from Allaah, and theirs will be a great torment.** ❖*-(Surah an-Nahl: 106)*

The people involved in these innovations should not say, our chests have been opened to embrace these matters you say are innovations, or our hearts are content with what we find with practicing them. Judging matters this way is not the true measure nor a sound standard by which we are able to judge what is correct. Rather the standard used must be the Book of Allaah, and the Sunnah of His Messenger, may the praise and salutations of Allaah be upon him. The measure is only what the Prophet proceeded upon and what his rightly guided successors proceeded upon of truth and guidance.

It is for this reason that the Prophet commanded the

Muslims to follow the sunnah of his rightly guided successors who would come after him, where he said, {Stick to my Sunnah and the sunnah of the rightly-guided Khaleefahs that come after me. Hold onto it and bite onto it with your molar teeth. And beware of newly invented matters, for indeed every newly-invented matter is an innovation and every innovation is a misguidance.}

The people involved and engaged in these innovations, whether they are general innovated paths and methodologies, or specific innovations restricted to matters of belief, if they return back to the truth of the original guidance they will find what better brings ease and contentment to them, and what cultivates comfort both within their hearts and in their behavior both.

This is through truly establishing and fulfilling the rights of Allaah, the rights of an individual himself to stand on true guidance, and the rights of the other worshippers generally, they will find contentment in that way which is in fact much better by far than what they experienced previously upon innovation. Then, it will become clear to them that what they previously proceeded upon was clearly wrongdoing and misguidance, and actually only an unrecognized trial and punishment for them."

It should be noted that the harm of those upon innovation includes others. Ibn al-Qayyim, may Allaah have mercy upon him, discussing the difference in the harm caused by the one sinning in matters of the religion and the one knowingly proceeding upon innovation in Islaam, said, [66]

"It is established and known that the sinner, primarily damages himself, as for the innovator he damages himself as well as other people.

The trial brought through the innovation is dangerously connected to the very roots of the religion, whereas the situation of the sinner is generally restricted to him being overcome by his own worldly desires.

The innovator is one who actually blocks people from proceeding upon the straight path of Allaah and prevents them from walking upon it, whereas the situation of the sinner is not usually to that degree of such harm to others.

The innovator may be someone who, due to innovated belief, speaks ill and defames affirmed descriptions of Allaah and what is related to His perfection above creation. Whereas the harm produced by the sinner is not of this central importance and significance.

The innovator opposes and contradicts that guidance brought by the Messenger of Allaah, whereas the sinner does not do this, but falls into following his worldly desires, despite acknowledging what is correct from guidance.

The innovators inevitably separate people from the only path leading them to be truly successful in the Hereafter. Whereas the sinner is, despite his sins which burden him down personally, is still himself slowly moving in that essential direction. "

The deviation and swerving from the straight path inevitably caused by involvement in innovations in the religion that were was not originally part of it, was a fact affirmed by all the leading scholars of the Salaf. Al-Hasan al-Basree, may Allaah have mercy upon him, from the prominent early scholars of Islaam, from the generation of the Successors to the Companions, said,[67]

---

[67] Narrated in Ibn Wadhaah in his 'al-Bid'ah wa Nahy anha' no. 69 with an sound chain of narration.

"The person upon innovation in the religion does not increase his efforts in his fasting and his prayer except that he only increases in distance from Allaah, due to his innovation."

There is no doubt that of those sins which a Muslim might commit innovation is from the most serious and severe, after major disbelief. For that reason it is important that we understand the significant danger there is an underlying misguidance found in the incorrect beliefs and principles which cause various groups, movements, and sects, to oppose the Sunnah and fight against the people who strive to adhere to it in their statements and actions. One of the most significant of these is related to innovating and altering the religion of Islaam through adding or removing new practices. Our sheikh the guiding scholar Sheikh Zayd Ibn Muhammad al-Madkhalee, may Allaah have mercy upon him, explained what would happen if various callers to Islaam turned away from their innovations, and focused upon calling to what the Companions and those who learned from them considered Islaam,[68]

"Indeed we say, and we seek refuge in Allaah from speaking with something which isn't correct, we say that if everyone involved in efforts intended to establish Islaam, established their efforts to call to Allaah, by proceeding in those efforts upon the specific way the scholars of the first three generations, truly following them in how they followed the path of the prophets and messengers in their methodology of calling humanity to Islaam, then through that adherence Allaah would open up the hearts of many of the people of discernment and intelligence, and many people would pay true attention with openness and receptiveness. Allaah has said, ﴾ So set you (O Muhammad) your face towards the religion of pure Islamic Monotheism Hanifa (worship none but Allaah Alone) Allaah's Fitrah, with which He has

[68] Terrorism: It's Harmful Results And Effects, page 14

created mankind... ❋ – *(Surah ar-Rum: 30)*

> *However, today these callers of different movements and groups have chosen and laid out for themselves, various devised methodologies which do not conform to the methodology of the scholars from the first three generations, which was followed by those Muslims throughout the centuries who proceeded upon their clear methodology in inviting to Allaah. Those who follow these deviated methodologies, deviated in relation to both the means they utilize and the goals they aim for in calling of Islaam, will not even lead to them achieving their objectives, as those goals actually destroys their strength and wastes their many efforts. And Allaah knows the reality of the true objectives of such people, and the actual direction and focus of their inner thoughts and intentions."*

Sheikh Muhammad Ibn Saaleh al-'Utheimeen, may Allaah have mercy upon him, was asked about innovating new methodologies in some aspects of how we practice Islaam, [69]

"What is the ruling regarding the concept of merging together conflicting understandings of Islaam? What is meant by this, is that an individual believes in the affirmed fundamental beliefs as held by the first generations, as perhaps he has studied and graduated from the College of Calling to Allaah, or the College of Sharee'ah, or the College of Hadeeth from one of our universities here in Saudi Arabia, for example. So generally he stands upon the methodology of the Salaf in beliefs, because he has studied this path or way of thinking transmitted from the first generations.

Yet when he approaches the realm or issue of calling to Allaah he says "No, not this previous methodology, as it does actually not benefit us. Rather we will follow

[69] Open Door Meetings Cassette number 128, Side B

a different methodology for this." Whether he intends by that alternate methodology, that of the organization of the Muslim Brotherhood, or the group Jama'at at-Tableegh, or that of some other group. He holds that, "Our following this other methodology in calling to Allaah will not harm us because our beliefs are those of the Salaf. But for the Salafee methodology of calling to Allaah then it is not appropriate or suitable for today." So the question is, did the first three generations make such a distinction between their basic beliefs and their methodology in calling to the religion? May Allaah bless you.

> *Answer: 'Minhaj', or methodology, may Allaah bless you, is built upon 'aqeedah', or beliefs. So without doubt, the one whose 'aqeedah' is sound, then his 'minhaj' will be sound. This is because the Prophet, may Allaah's praise and salutations be upon him, mentioned the dividing of this Muslim Ummah into seventy three sects, all of whom are in the fire except for one. They asked him, "Which is that oh Messenger of Allaah?" He replied, {**That one which is upon what I and my Companions are upon today.**" So his statement "**the one which is upon what I and my Companions are upon today**}, meaning in 'aqeedah', or beliefs, and 'minhaj', or methodology, various deeds, and in every other matter. Such that is it not possible that there be a true difference between this matter and the second.*

> *For example, those upon the way of the Muslim Brotherhood organization, or the way of the group Jamaa'at at-Tableegh, or those involved with calling in an effort to reform and correct our affairs, or any others, if their methodology did not differ with the revealed Sharee'ah then there would be no harm. Yet if there is any matter in their methodology which conflicts with the revealed Sharee'ah, then it is required that they turn*

*back, start again with, and give precedence to their
'aqeedah'. Because every action has its intention, and if
an individual embraces a methodology which conflicts
with the general methodology of the Messenger, upon
him be Allaah's praise and salutations, and that of the
rightly guided Khaleefahs who came after him, then the
meaning of this is that his beliefs are not sound and not
correct. Otherwise when his 'aqeedah' stands as sound
and correct then his 'minhaj', or methodology, would
also be correct.*

*As such it is necessary that I further say: from the
afflictions which characterize the present condition
of this Ummah, specifically in the present age, is our
obvious disunity and separation. Such that this person
is following the methodology devised by so and so, and
this other person is following this other methodology of so
and so. And if only they were leave this way of attaching
themselves to specific individuals and take Islaam
generally! Rather, what has occurred is that each such
person upon the methodology of so and so then declares
the others as astray, and perhaps even declares him a
disbeliever due to issues that there is no true evidence
that they are misguided in, nor is there present that
which truly indicates one's disbelief.*

*This state of trial and ordeal has struck a blow upon
the Islamic revival that we previously had such good
hopes for a few years ago because many of the youth have
now become divided and scattered. Perhaps one of them
might hate this other youth, who is his brother who only
desires the truth, just as he himself does, with a hatred
more severe than he would direct toward the person
who is an open evil doer! And we ask Allaah to grant us
health and well being in our affairs.*

All of what we have just described is from the inspiration of Shaytaan and his whispered commands. Therefore it is obligatory upon us to stand in accord with each other and to sit and investigate and scrutinize matters, such that the result is everyone supporting and defending anyone found to stand upon the truth, as well as us indicating and shedding light upon the one found to be upon falsehood.

Yet if someone from among us were to say, about a matter of differing, I do not understand in this issue other than that such and such statement is correct, while taking his position from the independent evidenced judgments put forth by a reliable scholar, as well as that position he holds is supported by the meanings of the Arabic language as well as the principles of the Sharee'ah- then regarding this individual we do not state that he proceeds upon misguidance. As then, all praise is due to Allaah, it is an issue of accepted legitimate evidenced differences from the scholars, which is extensive and encompassing."

Sheikh al-Albaanee, may Allaah have mercy upon him, explained about some Muslims who understand what is correct, and truly want good for others but do not always call others to it in the best of ways. At times this occurs towards the general Muslims who have simply been deceived by the claims of astray and misguided groups, without sufficient clarifications reaching them. He stated, may Allaah have mercy upon him, [70]

"...In comparison to those people to give absolutely no importance to ensuring their beliefs are correct or correcting the misconceptions of people generally, these other Muslims are the complete opposite of them, giving their full efforts to the necessity of learning and knowing the truth in those matters that the people differ about. However they oppose with the sternest opposition the

[70] Silsilaat al-Hudaa wa an-Nur audio tape series no. 10

negligent position of the first type of individuals, yet the correct position is found between this group and that group. As it is a requirement that we base our position towards the various groups within the boundaries of Islaam, upon affirming the general brotherhood among the believers. Such that if a Muslim comes to know from his Muslim brother some mistake, in fact if he sees from him more than one sin or fault, then it is not proper that he only take a position of enmity, rather he must advise him.

With his advice towards him being undertaken with that gentleness and wisdom which is commanded within the Book of Allaah and the Sunnah. ❧ **Invite mankind, O Muhammad to the Way of your Lord with wisdom (i.e. with the Divine Inspiration and the Qur'aan) and fair preaching, and argue with them in a way that is better.** ❧*-Surah an-Nahl: 125)*

As such it is only proper that those Muslims focused upon learning and knowing the truth in those matters that the people differ about, also recognize and acknowledge, about the rest of the people who are in the state of error, that they are like the person who is sick or ill. Meaning that what is required is that they be treated and helped by you, upon your having sincerity for Allaah's sake and using every suitable gentleness. It is not permissible that you just treat them harshly and roughly, because we know that Allaah, the Most Glorified and the Most Exalted, addressed his prophet, may Allaah's praise and salutations be upon him, saying, ❧ **And had you been severe and harsh hearted, they would have broken away from about you...**❧*-(Surah Aal-Imraan: 159)*

Our call which is directed and driven by adherence to the Book of Allaah and the Sunnah, upon the methodology of the righteous predecessors from the first three generations does not only adopt enmity and hostility regarding the general individuals from any group from the various groups among the Muslims. But our position is that we differ with them in some of their concepts and understandings, and the new methodologies which they have. Yet that deficient condition is from what makes it obligatory upon us to advise them, and invite them to what is correct in every matter that they have strayed away from, and become distant from, our clear straight way of Islaam which is the way of our Lord."

The Importance of Avoiding of trials and controversies

In consideration of the situation today where many young Muslims find themselves being flooded with different statements about issues from various directions on the internet, it is important mentions what our scholars indicate is a crucial safeguard for the well-being of the personal religion of a new Muslim or of a Muslim newly committed to practicing Islaam. That is the avoidance of harmful trials and controversies that distract you from gaining beneficial knowledge or acting upon it[71]. The esteemed Sheikh Sulaymaan 'Abaa al-Khayl, may Allaah preserve him, described trials that occur among the people as having four characteristics we should be aware of, [72]

"The first characteristic is that it will come forth as something beautified and attractive in the beginning or initial stages.

---

[71] For a comprehensive list of advices related to this subject please refer to the third course appendix 'Important Guidelines For Every Muslim In Our Age Of Numerous Trials And Difficulties' within the book "30 Days of Guidance: Cultivating The Character & Behavior of Islaam"

[72] From the lecture "The Reality of Trials and the Path to Be Protected from Them.

The second characteristic is the proper use of intellects and comprehension often disappears in the midst of them.

The third characteristic is that they spread quickly and are difficult to extinguish and bring to an end.

The fourth characteristic is that they truly require being suspicious of it in the initial stage and thereafter require weighing and contemplating their evidence in the end of the affair."

This is very important in relation to problems and disagreements that may come forth between those who adhere to the Sunnah. Our discerning scholars have stressed the importance of how to proceed in these situations. Sheikh Sulaymaan ar-Ruhaylee, may Allaah preserve him said,[73]

"It is obligatory upon us in these conditions of the current age that we give concern to what will strengthen our devotion to Allaah generally, what will increase the unity of our ranks as believers standing upon the worship of Allaah alone and His Prophet's Sunnah. We must be warned away from heedlessly throwing accusations at others, speaking without intelligent consideration, and proceeding in matters without considering the wisdom of our actions.

Furthermore it is obligatory that Muslims return every matter back to those who are appropriate to deal with it while refusing to accept the ways of those who are needlessly preoccupying others with our bitter world circumstances in order to achieve their corrupt aim of seeking to harm the body of the people of the Sunnah and weaken the reliance and trust among their ranks."

---

[73] From the Sheikh personal social media accounts

One of the serious harmful consequences of Muslims entering into controversies and disputing is the damage it does to the relations and brotherhood which should be between those striving to adhere to the Sunnah and the way of the Salaf. Sheikh Zayd Ibn Muhammad al-Madkhalee, may Allaah have mercy upon him, discussed this issue of the results of having unsupported bad suspicions in an explanation of the statement of the Messenger of Allaah, may Allaah's praise and salutations be upon him,[74]

"{If you openly show your suspicions of people, you will corrupt them.}

Meaning if you accuse someone from the people with an accusation that has no reality or basis to it, and you confront them in a negative manner and your suspicion about them is a bad, certainly this harms them. Because an individual does not like to hear accusations about his honor or about himself generally, but wants to hear good. And perhaps you further injure them when you have the bad suspicion of them and then approach them as if they were evil people. This may injure them to the point of actually corrupting them, such that they actually fall into that which you before suspected, and then commit that deed which is a transgression.

*However, for the people of goodness, having a good suspicion is an obligation. It is not permissible to have unfounded bad suspicions of them. Indeed Allaah has criticized the having of unfounded bad suspicion of the believers ❧... **and you did think an evil thought and you became a useless people going for destruction.**❧ - (Surah al-Fath: 12) So Allaah criticized and censured them because of this. And Allaah, how free from any imperfection is He, said: ❧**Oh you who believe! Avoid much suspicions, indeed some suspicions are sins.**❧ -*

---

[74] From his commentary of al-Adab al-Mufrad, vol. 1 pg. 279-280

(Surah al-Hujuraat: 12) Such that Allaah,, the Most Glorified and the Most Exalted, has prohibited having an unfounded bad suspicion of the people of goodness.

This is different than the case of the people of transgression and doing ill, as they are the people of evil and wrongdoing. They themselves have no personal reservations or concerns about committing wrong doing nor do they give any care or concern that others have a bad suspicion about them. This is regardless of whether they are the disbelievers, the people of innovation in Islaam, or those Muslims who openly commit prohibited acts. As Allaah has said that some suspicion is a sin, which itself indicated that some other types of suspicion which are done in the proper context and situation are in fact not considered a sin..."

This is in regard to Muslims generally, and our scholars explain that such unfounded suspicions are even worse when they are directed toward those known to be acknowledged scholars upon the Sunnah. In the disagreements and controversies that sometimes occur some Muslims wrongly believe that it is obligatory upon them and everyone to publicly chose a position between sides, speak about these controversies, and call others to their chosen position. This may lead others to enter these controversies, and increase the overall harm to the Muslims. One of the mistakes commonly seen in controversies is those who are not scholars begin putting forth statements in matters that should have been left to the scholars to eventually address, speak about, and strive to rectify in a way that they deem suitable. The guiding scholar Sheikh Sheikh Muhammad 'Amaan al-Jaamee, may Allaah have mercy upon him, discussed this saying,[75]

---

[75] From an audio file in the voice of the Sheikh, may Allaah have mercy upon him

"...None of these are from the proper behavior for calling to the religion, nor the behavior that rectifies affairs. It simply causes chaos, confusion, and provocation for the young Muslims. This is what I have previously said, and this is what I say now. And it is what I say for the future.

Those who should refute and debate are the scholars. So we advise our students to not enter the issues that arise between some of the students of knowledge and between the scholars. If a scholar makes a mistake, then the refutation will be from another scholar. But as for you, why do you tire yourself out with this, what do you gain from entering in the issues between the scholars. You only slip into backbiting, and blameworthy censure of the scholars and the students of knowledge.

So you do not truly benefit from it anything, in fact it causes your loss. Due to this we advise the Muslim youth to stay far away from being in this position, as it is not appropriate or suitable for them to enter into this."

Yet this brings us to an important question, how do those who are not scholars determine when they should put forth their position and what they see as correct? Sheikh Saaleh al-Fauzaan was in fact asked this, "**May Allaah increase you in good. How can we distinguish between being silent about tribulations which is something blameworthy, and between avoiding entering needlessly into trials which is something praiseworthy?** Sheikh Fauzaan, responded by saying, [76]

"As for trials, it is only for the people of knowledge and insight to speak during them. It is not for anyone and everyone to speak about such matters. Because when someone who is ignorant speaks during trials it only increases the trial and its harm. Whereas when the scholars speak, clarifying and explaining, it causes the

---

[76] From an audio file in the voice of the Sheikh, may Allaah preserve him

trial to lesson and die down, by Allaah's permission.

So, it is not for anyone and everyone to speak about such matters, rather the ones who should speak during them are the people of knowledge and insight. Those who comprehend the truth from falsehood, and understand how to speak in a way that benefits. But it is not the case that every individual should delve into trials, speaking, and making pronouncements and saying this and that, yes."

Sheikh 'Ubayd al-Jaabiree, may Allaah preserve him, mentioned within a lecture "The Causes Or Reasons For Being Safe And Successful When Trials Occur" that when trials or an incident occurs among the Muslims and some of the people of knowledge make a statement regarding it, while others have not yet spoken such that you could also know their own position or assessment, then it is necessary for the young Muslims to not act hastily in the matter, acting in a way that brings a knife of anger down on some of their brothers. Rather, what is upon them is to look and investigate closely what the contemporaries and associates of those scholars who have already spoken also say in the matter, meaning their companions in knowledge. They should investigate from other scholars who are brothers and contemporaries to the first steadfast scholars, in order to strive to find out their positions in the affair, as they are also from the scholars. Furthermore, Sheikh al-'Utheimeen, may Allaah have mercy upon him, said,[77]

"It is upon the students of knowledge to honor the scholars, acknowledge their status, and open their hearts, by acting graciously, towards whatever differences occur between the scholars and others. The must face this situation by excusing the scholar who proceeded in a way that leads to making a mistaking in a matters of beliefs. This is a very

[77]   Majmu'a al-Fataawa vol.26 pgs. 90-92

important point. Because some of the people follow and pursue the mistake of others, in order to take from what was found a conclusion which is not suitable in regard to that person. Then they proceed to cause confusion and disturb the people who listen to the person whose mistakes they pursued. This is from the most significant of mistakes and errors. Since, if backbiting and gossiping about a general Muslim is considered from the major sins, then the gossiping and backbiting of a scholar is even greater and more significant that!

As when someone wrongfully backbites a scholar, the harm caused by this is not confined to that scholar, rather it harms both him and that Sharee'ah knowledge he carries and transmits. This is due to the fact that for the general people, if a scholar is diminished in their eyes and dropped in their estimation, then his words and statements are dropped also. Such that if he was someone stating the truth and guiding others to it, the backbiting by this person of a scholar then becomes a barrier and obstacles to that Sharee'ah knowledge he possesses. Therefore the danger of doing so is greater and more significant.

As such I say, it is necessary that the young men deal with what occurs of differences or disagreements between the scholars upon assuming the best intention, and upon acknowledging that it is in areas requiring their independent scholastic assessments, and so they should excuse those scholars for whatever mistakes they made. Additionally, there is nothing preventing you from speaking with these scholars about those matters which you believe they are mistaken in, to determine whether the mistake is actually from them or from those who have claimed that the scholar made a mistake. As sometimes a person will incorrectly perceive that the statement of a scholar is wrong, yet after discussion with him, one comes to realize that it was actually correct.

*Moreover, every person is human, the Prophet said, {**All of the sons of Adam make mistakes, and the best of those who make mistakes are those who repent from them.**} As for the person who becomes wrongly pleased when he sees the slip or mistake that a scholar makes, due to the opportunity to circulate it and spread it among the people, such that separation and spliting results, then this is not from the way of the Salaf, the first three generations. Similarly, this is also the case with the errors and sins that come from the Muslim rulers and governing leaders. It is not permissible for us to utilize those things in which they are wrong as a means to disparage and speak against them generally about everything, disregarding what good they have put forth.*

*As Allaah states in His Book, ◌ **O you who believe! Stand out firmly for Allaah and be just witnesses and let not the enmity and hatred of others make you avoid justice. Be just: that is nearer to piety, and fear Allaah. Verily, Allaah is Well-acquainted with what you do**. ◌-(Surah al-Ma'idah: 8) By this meaning, do not allow your hatred or dislike of some people to prevent you from being just and fair. As acting with justice and fairness is obligatory, it is not permissible for someone to simply take the mistakes and shortcoming of one of the Muslims rulers or one of the scholars, or others, and spread them among the people, then also remain silent about the good they have done, as this is not from acting with fairness and justice."*

Certainly, we should never forget that Allaah will bring us forth to   bear witness against ourselves, for any wrongdoing, injustice, and oppression brought to other

Muslims without just cause by what our tongues produce. Allaah, the Most High, said, ❦ *It will be said to him: "... You yourself are sufficient as a reckoner against you this Day."* ❦-(Surah al-Isra':14). Sheikh al-'Utheimeen, may Allaah have mercy upon him, said in his commentary of this verse,[78]

> *"Some of the Muslims of the first three generations would say,* **'By Allaah, who could be more just to you than the one who makes you reckoner to judge and assess your own self.**" *And this is something true, from the truest forms of justice is that an individual is presented his own book of full accounting and it is said to him, 'You assess and reckon yourself according to what you have put forth.'"*

However, it is also important to understand that one mistake does not justify another opposing mistake. As a second mistake that some fall into in reaction to controversies is the rejection of evidenced clarifications from the scholars generally, despite the important role they play in preserving and protecting Islaam. The avoidance of delving into controversies should not lead a striving Muslim to an opposing mistake of dismissing the scholastic efforts of acknowledged scholars to refute and clarify mistakes and errors connected to Islaam and its practice, even those directed at the students and scholars of the people of the Sunnah. Rather it should encourage them to suffice themselves with the statements made by acknowledged scholars regarding that affair. As, since the age of the Companions, the scholars upon the Sunnah have never stopped refuting and clarifying mistakes of others whether outside or within the Muslim Ummah upon valid evidences, good manners, and in conformance with the guidelines and goals of Islaam. Included within their efforts are their criticisms and refutations of other

---

[78] Sharh as-Safaareenah, pg. 424

well-known scholars. This is done both in terms of larger issues of methodology as well as secondary very specific fiqh and jurisprudence rulings that were considered to be incorrect.

Understanding this is truly important because from the blameworthy excuses that are often used for not accepting, or denying evidence of issues that scholars have put forward are [You are only attacking the people of guidance!][79] and [This is only from the statements of criticism that have been distorted by personal differences among those who are contemporaries to one another!] However, even though this second claim may be true in some cases, asserting this absolutely is incorrect and not what the steadfast scholars upon the methodology of the Salaf state and adhere to. Rather, as part of their role in the Muslim Ummah, they specifically examine the evidences carefully and offer detailed affirmation or rejection of scholastic criticisms. This was explained by Sheikh Saaleh al-Fauzaan may Allaah preserve, was asked,[80] *May Allaah bless you with good, our esteemed sheikh, today whenever one scholar refutes the mistake of another, some of the people say "This is only what is known as the statements of contemporaries, which is put to the side not considered valid nor conveyed." What is your position, about this claim? Should it be accepted generally?*

"I will explain this matter to you, it is obligatory that you make the truth clear. It is required that you clarify the truth and refute errors or mistakes in the religion. We don't offer empty compliments to anyone, nor do we offer false flattery to anyone. Rather make clear the error or mistake, and indicate the truth of the matter which stands

[79] Fro a more detailed clarification of this misconception please refer to Lesson 19: Scholars Clarifying Errors Of Other Scholars Is Only Giving Advice from the book "An Educational Course Based Upon: Beneficial Answers to Questions On Innovated Methodologies By the Guiding Scholar Sheikh Saaleh Ibn Fauzaan al-Fauzaan (may Allaah preserve him) Twenty Lessons on The Knowledge, Beliefs, & Methodology of Islaam"

[80] An audio file in the sheikh's voice taken from www.alfawzan.ws

in contrast to that mistake. Yes, as our concern is not to worry about so-and so and such and such. Additionally, silence about such mistakes is not permissible. Because if we were to turn away from this mistake, and then a second mistake, and then a third mistake, then these many mistakes would start to be accepted, as the people falsely perceive that the silence of the scholars about these errors, is a proof that there is nothing wrong about them.

So it is required that these matters of error be made clear and explained, especially if they come from one who was has standing, from someone who is taken as an example by the people, or by someone who holds a position of leadership. Then the issue is even more dangerous, and so it must be addressed and clarified.

The error should be explained, whatever the situation. Meaning, do not allow people to be deceived by it. Yes, do not wrongly say, [Put this clarification to the side without considering it valid or conveying it to others.] This is a false statement. As the one who narrated something which is false or an error, and he is refuted and criticized, then whoever is displeased by this is displeased, and whoever is pleased with this is pleased. As our goal and focus is only the truth. Yes. Our goal is not to merely oppose individuals, and simply criticize and disparage people."

May Allaah preserve and lengthen his life, Sheikh al-Fauzaan, also explained that public evidenced clarifications are not only for those upon clear innovation among the Muslims,[81]

"...Additionally this affair is not restricted only to innovators in the religion. Rather it encompasses those who remain silent about such innovators. It also

---

[81] From A Valued Gift for the Reader Of Comments Upon the Book Sharh as-Sunnah, pg. 115

includes censuring and criticizing such people, because it is obligatory to explain and clarify these matters to the people, and this is the function served by knowledge based refutations available in the bookstores of the Muslims. These works of refutation defend the straight path and warn against the like of such misguided individuals as were mentioned....

Our goal is only the truth, not merely criticizing others, or simply speaking badly about the people, the goal is the clarification of what is indeed the truth. And this is the trust and duty which Allaah has laid upon the scholars. Such that silence is not permissible regarding individuals such as we have mentioned. But with great regret, if a scholar comes and refutes the like of such individuals, some people say [This is recklessness!] and other statements like this of deceptive whispers. But the people of knowledge have never failed to continue clarifying to the people the evil of misguided individuals, those who are callers to falsehood, they have never ceased doing so."

Indeed this is from the methodology of the guiding Imaams of our time. Imaam 'Abdul-'Azeez Ibn 'Abdullah Ibn Baaz, would examine books himself or at times have the works of others known to be upon the Sunnah examined by other steadfast scholars, such as Sheikh 'Abdul-'Azeez ar-Raajhee, may Allaah preserve him, when he, Sheikh Ibn Baaz, was unable to dedicate the time to examine them himself. He did this in order to take their assessment and, if needed, make any corrections from the aspect of sound Sharee'ah knowledge. This is shown in the following letter, [82]

---

[82] As mentioned in the introduction of the book itself, 'The Methodology of the People of Sunnah and the Jama'ah in Criticizing Individuals, Books, and Groups'

"From 'Abdul-'Azeez Ibn 'Abdullah Ibn Baaz to the honorable and noble brother and companion, the esteemed scholar Sheikh Rabee'a Ibn Haadee al-Madkhalee, may Allaah guide him to every matter which pleases Him, and further increase him in knowledge and faith, ameen.

Assalaamu 'aleikum wa rahmatAllaahi wa barakatuhu. As for what follows:

I am sending you as an attachment the response I received from the noble Sheikh 'Abdul-'Azeez Ibn 'Abdullah ar-Raajhee regarding your book, 'The Methodology of the People of the Sunnah and the Jama'ah in Criticizing Individuals, Books, and Groups'.

I had submitted it to him, due to not being able to complete its review personally. All praise is due to Allaah, he answered regarding his views regarding the work, and indeed his favorable answer pleased me; therefore I wanted to inform you of this.

I ask Allaah to make us and you and the rest of our brothers callers to the truth, and those who support the truth. Certainly, He is the Bountiful and Generous."

Sheikh Rabee'a ibn Haadee, may Allaah preserve him, himself shows this practically in relation to the scholastic refutations, by scholars upon the way of the Salaf, of specific positions taken by Sheikh al-Albaanee, may Allaah have mercy upon him, supporting both the scholars in their efforts of refuting those positions and those specific scholastic refutations. He stated clearly, [83]

"...Ninth: We support and confirm those who have refuted specific mistakes of Sheikh al-Albaanee or the mistakes of others. Because this is the truth. And you do

---

[83] The Overwhelming Falsehoods of 'Abdul-Lateef Bashmeel, pg.6

not have any knowledge that there has come forth from us, all praise is due to Allaah, the appearance of having blind partisanship towards any mistake from anyone- no matter who he may be. And anyone who claims that we stand upon other than this position, then indeed he is an open liar....

.....Firstly we, the scholars of Medina, affirm these scholars in every matter in which they were correct in their refutations of Sheikh al-Albaanee. This is because we proceed upon the methodology of the righteous Salaf, due to the fact that found within this methodology is the clear belief that the speech of everyone has within it that which is accepted and that which is rejected- except the Messenger of Allaah, may Allaah's praise and salutations be upon him.

As such, all of these scholars who have put forth refutations of positions of Sheikh al-Albaanee are indeed our scholars, beloved to us, and presently our associates, except those of them who have already died. Indeed I have myself also put forth refutations of the most crucial mistakes of Sheikh al-Albaanee such as the issue of seeking military assistance of the disbelievers due to necessity and in the issue of the oath of allegiance, and other matters."

Sheikh Muhammad Ibn Saaleh al-'Utheimeen responded to a questioner who asked, ***"Has the sunnah or practice of criticizing and commending individuals in the religion died and ceased? And what is the ruling regarding refuting the one who has contradicted something from the guidance of Islaam due to hating to enter into examining him or looking at him personally."*** He responded saying, [84]

---

[84]   Source Audio file in the voice of Sheikh Muhammad Ibn Saaleh al-'Utheimeen

"I fear that this statement is a true word by which falsehood is intended. As all praise is due to Allaah, the practice of criticism and commendation of individuals has not died, nor has it been buried, nor has not become feeble and sick. It is present and established. Indeed the practice of criticism and commendation of individuals is found within the evaluating of those witnesses who testify in front of the judge in court, as perhaps individuals testifying in a case may be questionable or unconfirmed, and so they seek clarifying testimony from them; and it is also used within the area of transmission of reports of religious knowledge. Certainly we just listened to the rectification of the imaam of the statement of Allaah, the Most High; ﴾ **Oh you who believe! If a rebellious evil person comes to you with a news, verify it** ﴿ *-(Surah al-Hujuraat: 6)*

Consequently, the practice of criticizing and commending individuals remains present as long as individuals of different types of acceptability will be found, as long as individuals of different levels of reliability will be found- the practice of criticizing and commending individuals will remain.

However, I fear that someone might say for instance that "This specific individual has been criticized." When he has not in fact been criticized. Such that they will take this apparent ruling as a means to spread and attribute faults to the people. For this reason I say, if an individual has a specific fault and there is a need for, a demand for, or it is seen that the overall benefit lies in clarifying his fault specifically and particularly; then there is no harm in this, certainly there is no harm in doing this. However, it is better that one would say: "Some people have done such and such criticized action" or "Some people have said such and such criticized statement". And this is for two reasons:

The first reasons is it is free from the issues related to specifying someone particularly.

And the second reason is that then the clarification is a general judgment upon him as well as others who are similar to him.

With the exception of the case when we see that a specific person has caused trials among the people, and he calls to innovation, and invites towards misguidance, then in this case it is required that we specifically identify him, in order that the people are not deceived by him."

Sheikh al-'Utheimeen, may Allaah have mercy upon him, discusses some false restrictions and conditions, which do not have any basis in the Sharee'ah, that are used to turn people away from evidenced detailed clarifications of mistakes of callers, students of knowledge, and of scholars upon the Sunnah. One of these false restrictions is that for refutations which originate from steadfast acknowledged scholars, it is required to mention an individual's good as well as his mistakes. He stated,[85]

"...Listen to me, young man, in the situation of refuting it is not suitable that I mention the merits of the individual I am refuting. If I were to mention that individual's merits, while I am refuting him, then this weakens my refutation of his error.

Questioner: Even when dealing with the people of the Sunnah our sheikh?

Sheikh al-'Utheimeen: This is in relation to both the people of the Sunnah as well as other than them. As

---

[85] From a transcript transmitted by Sheikh Rabee'a al-Madkhalee in his book 'A Defense Against the Aggressions of Adnan Against the Scholars of the Sunnah and al-Emaan'

when I am putting forth a refutation, how could it be that I am refuting someone and I start to bring forth his praise and merits? Is this sensible?"

This is and will remain the way of the people of the Sunnah between negligence and extremism. Indeed Ibn al-Qayyim transmitted a statement from al-Hasan al-Basree, may Allaah have mercy upon him, saying,[86]

"The Sunnah, I swear by the One whom there is none worthy of worship other than Him, stands between the one who goes to an extreme and the one who is negligent. So be patient upon it, may Allaah have mercy upon you, since the people of the Sunnah where few among the people in the ages that have passed, and they will remain few among the people in the time that remains of this world.

They are those who do not move with the people of destruction in their destruction and ruining of the religion, nor move with the people of innovation in their transgressing into innovation, but remain patient upon the Sunnah until they meet their Lord. So you all should be this way, if Allaah so wills."

---

[86] Ighaathat al-Lahafaan: vol. 1 pg. 70

In closing it is important to mention that there are few blessings that compare to the strength of emaan or faith in Allaah that Allaah places in one of His worshippers' hearts and His guiding them to embrace and chose to walk upon His straight path, especially for the one who embraces Islaam from people upon disbelief. They are blessed with understanding that true message which every prophet brought to humanity. Ibn Taymeeyah, may Allaah have mercy upon him, said,[87]

> *"The reality of the religion of Islaam is found in completely submitting to Allaah, and not to anyone other than him. This is the meaning of "There is none worthy of worship except Allaah."*

He also transmitted a statement from al-Hasan al-Basree,[88] may Allaah have mercy upon him, explaining that there are different kinds of knowledge,

> *"As such it has been said that there are two categories of knowledge, knowledge that is within the heart and knowledge which is on the tongue. The knowledge which is in the heart is what is considered beneficial knowledge, while the knowledge which is only of the tongue is a proof in front of Allaah against the worshippers."*

Ibn Taymeeyah, may Allaah have mercy upon him, explained that truly beneficial knowledge will enable us to establish that key relationship with Allaah before all else,[89]

> *"The heart will not be rectified, nor reach a condition of success and safety, nor be at ease and be in an overall good state, nor be truly tranquil and generally satisfied except through fulfilling the worship of its Lord, loving Him, seeking and turning to Him for assistance in their*

---

[87] Majmu' al-Fataawa vol. 4 pg. 245 Majmu'a al-Fataawa: vol. 9, pg. 379
[88] As narrated in Sunan ad-Daaramee vol.1 pg. 102
[89] Majmu'a al-Fataawa vol.10 pg. 194

affairs. Such that even if a created worshiper gains every matter of help that brings security the creation is capable of offering him, he will not reach ease nor gain a true state of satisfaction while his heart remains in need of the essential connection to its Lord."

Sheikh al-'Utheimeen, may Allaah have mercy upon him, also described an aspect of this saying,[90]

"Faith has a sweetness and a taste that will not be experienced except by the one whom Allaah bestows His mercy upon, through being granted this sweetness and this taste."

From the earlier scholars of the Ummah, Muhammad Ibn Sireen, may Allaah have mercy upon him, said,[91]

"If Allaah wants good for a servant He placed for him within his heart a warner and reminder which commands him towards goodness and prohibits him from wrongdoing."

Similarly, from the later scholars of the Ummah, Haafidh Ibn Katheer, may Allaah have mercy upon him, stated, in his famous work explaining the Qur'aan,[92]

"The one who fears Allaah by fulfilling His commands and by turning away those matters He has prohibited, is directed towards understanding and distinguishing between what is the truth and what is falsehood."

Likewise, from the verifying senior scholars of the Ummah, Sheikh al-'Utheimeen, may Allaah have mercy upon him, reminded us that,[93]

"The one who has a pure heart, then Allaah, the Most High, may endow him with inner insight through which he comes to recognize sins, such that within himself he

---

[90] From his explanation of Kitaab al-Tawheed: vol.3, pg. 180
[91] az-Zuhd: narration 1791
[92] Tafseer Ibn Katheer. vol. 4 pg. 43
[93] From his explanation of Bulugh al-Maraam, vol. 2 pg. 249

is not satisfied nor pleased with something. This matter is something which is a blessing from Allaah upon a person."

But it is important to understand that the opposite also occurs, and is a real possibility, a danger we face, and which we have been warned of. Ibn Jawzee, may Allaah have mercy upon him, said,[94]

"There are four matters that you should never approach, major disbelief, innovating in the religion, committing sins, and heedlessness. This is my advice which I present to you."

The guiding scholar Ibn al-Qayyim, may Allaah have mercy upon him said,[95]

"Sins in relation to their effect upon the heart are like poison. Even if it does not kill it, severely weakens it, such that it inevitably weakens its strength to the point that it is not able to resist being infected by other diseases."

He, may Allaah have mercy upon him, explained this in detail saying in his work al-Fawaa'id,

"From the results of us committing sins is a decrease in the success we are blessed with, that our views and perspectives become corrupted, that the truth becomes less apparent to us, that our hearts become corrupted and we become lazy in engaging in the remembrance of Allaah, that we waste time and become distant from the righteous in creation. From them is alienation and a distance grows between a worshiper and his Lord, that our supplications are prevented from being answered, that our hearts become hardened, the blessing which is found in our livelihood and time is lost, that we are deprived from gaining beneficial knowledge, and so clothed in humiliation."

[94] at-Tadhkirah: pg. 184
[95] Za'd al-Ma'aad: vol. 4 pg. 186

The dangers of simply neglecting guidance that gives life to our heart as a Muslim are also mentioned by him, may Allaah have mercy upon him, in his work al-Waabil as-Sayyib,

> *"When the heart becomes rusty, it no longer has the general nature of recognizing matters for what they truly are. Perhaps it will see what is falsehood and wrongly imagine it to be the truth, and likewise view what is from the truth and consider it to be a form of falsehood."*

This important understanding is also pointed out by those among leading scholars of this century, such as Sheikh al-'Utheimeen, may Allaah have mercy upon him, who explained that,[96]

> *"The involvement of wrongdoing and sins has a strong effect upon the heart. That which has the severe effect is the following of desires which are worse than doubts and misconceptions. As misconceptions are actually easier to remedy for the one whom Allaah makes that easy, since their source is ignorance which is addressed and treated by learning and study.*
>
> *But as for the following of desires, it is from an individual wanting what is wrong or falsehood. As such is it an affliction that destroys both the one who has gained a degree of knowledge as well as the general person who is ignorant."*

Alhamdulillah, the cures and remedies of diseases of the heart as found in the Sunnah are straightforward and clear. Ibn 'Awn, may Allaah have mercy upon him, said, [97]

> *"The remembering and focusing on people is a disease and ailment, and the remembering and focusing upon Allaah is a cure and remedy.*

---

[96] Majmu'a al-Fataawa: vol. 9, pg. 379
[97] Siyaar 'Alaam an-Nubala vol. 6 pg. 396

Imaam adh-Dhahabee, may Allaah have mercy upon him said, "Yes, by Allaah, I am shocked at us and our ignorance, how we abandon the cure and turn away from the remedy, and rather rush to engage and delve deep into the sickness or ailment. Allaah the Most High says,

❧ **Those who believe (in the Oneness of Allaah - Islamic Monotheism), and whose hearts find rest in the remembrance of Allaah, Verily, in the remembrance of Allaah do hearts find rest.** ❧ *-(Surah ar-Ra'd: 28)...*

...But someone cannot be truly prepared to do so except through being given success in that by Allaah, and by continually turning to the mentioned cure of His remembrance, as it is necessary to knock on a door if you expect it to open."

As Ibn al-Qayyim mentions that Rabee'a Ibn Anas, may Allaah have mercy upon him, said,[98]

"From the signs of loving Allaah is frequently remembering and mentioning him, since someone does not love something except that they mention it often. "

al-Haafidh Ibn Rajab, may Allaah have mercy upon him, said,[99]

"Being preoccupied with cleaning and purifying our hearts is better that engaging in frequent fasting and ritual Prayer, when the state of someone is one of self-deception and being beguiled."

Ibn al-Qayyim, may Allaah have mercy upon him, stated that,[100]

"Remembrance of Allaah is a healing for the heart, and its medicine, where neglecting and being heedless of this

---

[98] Madaarij as-Saalikeen, vol. 2 pg. 163
[99] Lataa'if al-Ma'aareefah, pg. 427
[100] al-Waabil as-Sayyib, pg. 172

if what causes it to be ill. Since the healing and the treatment of the hearts is found within the practice of legislated statements of dhikr or remembrance of Allaah, the Most High."

We can see the importance of understanding this as the guided Muslims have always understood this in the explanation of the verse, ❧ *And remember your Lord by your tongue and within yourself, humbly and with fear without loudness in words in the mornings, and in the afternoons and be not of those who are neglectful.*❧–(Surah al-A'raf: 205) The guiding scholar Imaam as-Sa'dee, may Allaah the Most High, have mercy upon him, said in explaining this verse,[101]

> *"The remembrance of Allaah, the Most High, may be done within the heart, or it may be done with the tongue, or may be performed with both at the same time, this last being the most complete form of dhikr and most excellent of its types. Allaah originally first commanded His worshipper and Messenger Muhammad with this remembrance, and then commanded others from the believers with it afterwards, meaning that they engage in remembrance of their Lord purely and sincerely for Him alone.*
>
> *The word ❧humbly❧ means humbly with your tongue, repeating the various authentic phrases of remembrance. The words ❧with fear❧ means within your heart with it having fear of Allaah, focusing your heart significantly upon Him, having a fear that your actions of worship might not be acceptable. A related sign of this inward fear is that you strive and struggle diligently in perfecting your worship for Allaah, sincerely advising yourself to correct it, working to cultivate it to be in the best of states and forms possible as His worshiper.*

---

[101] Tayseer al-Kareem ar-Rahman 1:314

The word ❁*without loudness in words*❁ meaning that it be done in a balanced moderate way. Not that your prayers to him be openly audible, nor be simply unheard whispers, but that you strive to offer it upon a way between both of these ways.

The word ❁*in the mornings*❁ meaning in the early part of the day.

The words ❁*and in the afternoons*❁ means in the later part of the day. These two times generally have a distinct virtue and advantage over other times.

The words ❁*and be not of those who are neglectful*❁ meaning those who forget about Allaah and so were made to forget themselves. By falling into this neglect they prevent themselves from gaining goodness both in this world and the next of the Hereafter. They are turning away from every form of goodness and content that is gained through remembrance and pure worship of Allaah alone. Just as they are falling towards every kind of misery, and every form of frustrating failure due to that which they have occupied themselves with instead of it.

For this reason implementing this guidance is from the most essential of the manners which the sincere worshipper must give attention to realizing and safeguarding, such that he spends significant time in the remembrance of Allaah during the night as well as the day. This especially in the last parts of the night, undertaken with sincere humbleness fearing his Lord, submissively quiet, repeatedly engaging in remembrance with both his heart and tongue with the proper manners and reverence. And that he dedicates himself to making supplications and remembrance, bridling his heart, and not being neglectful of it, as Allaah does not answer the *supplications coming from that heart which is heedless of him."*

Ibn al-Qayyim, may Allaah the Most High have mercy uponhim,[102]

"Engaging in statements of dhikr or remembrance gives the one doing so strength, such that he is able to accomplish through joining remembrance to his actions that which he is normally unable to accomplish. Indeed, I have witnessed this strength from Sheikh al-Islaam Ibn Taymeeyah, may Allaah have mercy upon him, in his walking, speech, writing and general courage something which is amazing. He would be able to write in a single day a work that which a scribe would not be able to complete within an entire week or more. The soldier who fought with him during a battle saw this similar incredible effect in what he was able to undertake at that time.

*Indeed, the Prophet, may the praise and salutations of Allaah be upon him, taught his daughter and her husband 'Alee, may Allaah be pleased with both of them, to every time they lay down on their bed, to say subhanAllaah thirty three times, say alhamdulillah thirty three times, and then say Allaahu akbar thirty four times, when they asked him for a servant to help them, as they had complained to him of the difficulties they were enduring working with grinding grain, labor, and necessary hard work, and so he taught them this practice of dhikr. He said to them, {**This is better for you than having a servant.**} It has been said, "That the one who is consistent in that will find a strength in his body that suffices from needing a servant."*

---

[102] al-Waabil as-Sayyib, pg. 185

If we take these many jewels from the people of the Sunnah that are plentiful, we will be equipping ourselves to be successful in both this world and the next, by Allaah's permission. We should never forget that as Sheikh al-Fauzaan, may Allaah preserve him, reminds us,[103]

"On the Day of Resurrection nothing will remain with you except your good deeds. The wealth you possess will not remain with you, your close relatives will not remain with you, nor your children, nor any of your brothers."

Sheikh Zayd Ibn Muhammad al-Madkhalee, may Allaah have mercy upon him, said, [104]

"It is obligatory upon a Muslim to know that righteous deeds and actions are a cause for entering into Paradise, and that evil actions and deeds are a cause for entering Hellfire. So they must ask from Allaah the guidance of having hearts which are sincere, truthful, and accepting of the truth, and ask that they be guided upon the path of guidance as Muslims.

He should seek to establish the obligatory duties to Allaah as He has legislated for them, and strive to further gain closeness to Allaah through additional acts of worship, and recommended deeds with their body and their wealth.

He should utilize his tongue in putting forth statements of truth, engaging in the remembrance of Allaah, reciting the Qur'aan, and rectifying affairs and reconciling between different Muslims, and similar actions from righteous endeavors and undertakings. It is also upon him to be careful and stay away from being resentful and discontented with Allaah in either his statements or actions. We ask Allaah to bless us with Jannah, and we seek refuge in Him from Hellfire. Indeed He is the One

[103] Explanation of the work Dala'il an-Nabuwaah page 201
[104] al-Irshaad Ilaa Tawdheeh Lama'at al-Itiqaa'd, pg 116

who hears and responds to our supplications."

I ask Allaah to make this effort from my sincere good deeds. It is also essential to thank and ask Allaah to reward the many scholars and students of knowledge whose beneficial works I quoted and referred to in an effort to make this and other course books beneficial. May Allaah increase their rewards and forgive them and us and enter us all into His Jannah. It should be noted that this course is compiled by a student, therefore the shortcomings or errors within should be referred to our noble scholars for clarification, as well as brought to the attention of the publisher as sincere advice so that the evidenced corrections or obligatory amendments that the scholars indicated can be made in future editions.[105]

In closing it is important to remind my brothers and sisters, that just as our noble scholar Sheikh Muhammad Baazmool, may Allaah preserve him, stated, I say,[106]

"I am deficient, and I openly admit that, in order that no one might wrongly suppose that in terms of what I have written, I comprehend and understand it completely, as having deficiencies and shortcomings are part of my general nature. I ask Allaah for help, assistance, guidance, direction, and success...

...No one should imagine that I fully embody what I have written, in terms of its completeness. As what I write and put forward is what I aspire towards for myself, and what I also desire for others from among my brothers. I hope for that goodness for all of us. This is what I advise them towards, just as I would like the

---

[105] Although we often are not able to respond and offer thanks, correspondence with constructive evidenced corrections or beneficial comments from those who have used this course are welcomed, and the senders are thanked for their sincere advice. These can be sent to:

Taalib al-Ilm Educational Resources
P.O. Box 27
Unityville, PA 17774, USA

[106] From the Facebook page of Sheikh Muhammad Baazmool

same, from them, directed towards me. I ask Allaah to grant all of us success in being guided to what He loves and is pleased with."

Likewise, I say as our dear and noble sheikh the guiding senior scholar Sheikh Ahmad Ibn Yahya an-Najmee, may Allaah have abundant mercy upon him, has stated in his introduction to the book 'al-Fataawa al-Jaleeyah' part 2,

"I do not free myself from committing mistakes in this work, as indeed no one is free of this. And I hope from the noble reader that if he encounters something that is obligatory to warn about that they should draw my attention to that as someone whom indeed I would thank, and that they inform me of that mistake, clarifying to me what exactly is the mistake in what was stated and how it conflicts with Sharee'ah evidences. As the brother who advises me will find me as one who submits and yields to the truth, turning towards it.

That which I do request from the reader is that they offer supplications for me in my absence.[107] As indeed I am in need of such supplications, that Allaah forgive me sins, and that He give me insight into my shortcomings, and that He bless me with steadfastness upon the truth until I meet him as one clinging even to the very edges of the Sunnah, having proceeded upon the straight methodology and way, and having placed my reliance upon the Most Gracious, the Most Merciful."

---

[107] The permissibility of requesting someone living to supplicate for you when done in conformity with the guidelines of the Sharee'ah has been established clearly by the texts of the Qur'aan and Sunnah as explained by the guiding scholars. This is seen in ruling no. 11613 by the Permanent Committee for Scholastic Research & Rulings when they were asked: **What is your view of the one who when someone is leaving him he says to him, "Do not forget me in your supplications." or if that other person is going to Mecca he says to him, "Make supplications for me brother." Is this permissible?**
The answer: It is permissible for a Muslim to request from his brother Muslims that he supplicate for him when traveling to perform 'Umraah or traveling for other reasons. This is only recommending and advising with that which contains good. And the success is from Allaah. May the praise and salutation of Allaah be upon our Prophet, his household, and his Companions.

That which is correct from my efforts as a student is from the guidance of Allaah and only through His mercy, and that which is deficient is only from myself and Shaytaan, the accursed enemy of those who believe.

May the praise and salutations of Allaah be upon the Messenger of Allaah, his household, his Companions, and all those who followed his guidance until the Day of Judgment. And all praise is due to Allaah alone, Lord of all the worlds.

Abu Sukhailah Khalil Ibn-Abelahyi
Taalib al-Ilm Educational Resources
the 9th of Rabee'a al-Aakheer, 1440 -
(Corresponding to December 16th, 2018)

(1)

GUIDING ADVICE ABOUT PROCEEDING IN LIFE FROM AN SENIOR SCHOLAR

In the name of Allaah, the Most Gracious, the Most Merciful

From Muhammad Ibn Saaleh al-'Utheimeen, to his (religious) son from among the young Muslims, may Allaah, the Most High, preserve and protect him.

Assalaamu 'aleikum wa rahmatAllaahi wa barakatuhu,

As for what follows: Certainly, you have requested from me, may Allaah bless you, to clarify the best way in which you should proceed in your life. So I ask Allaah, the Most High, to grant us all success to be directed to that which is His guidance, what is proper, righteousness, correct, and truly suitable. And I ask that He makes us of those who are guided and guide others to the truth, those who are righteous and enable righteousness and others. So I say:

Firstly, in relation to your relationship with Allaah, the Most Glorified and the Most Exalted:

1- Strive to always be a person who is with Allaah, the Most Glorified and the Most Exalted, as someone cognizant and aware of His transcendence and glory. Be an individual who thinks and ponders over the physical signs of His glory, such as the creation of the heavens and earth, and what resides in both of these regions of creation. As these are signs of the fullness and completeness of His wisdom, the magnificence of His strength and ability, and the tremendous scope of His mercy and favors upon us. As well as considering the sign of the excellence of revealed ways of guidance which He sends His messengers with, especially that of the final and seal of the messengers, <u>Muhammad, m</u>ay Allaah's praise and salutations be upon him.

2- Strive to bring your heart to a state in which it is filled with the love of Allaah, the Most High, due to the numerous blessings which are bestowed upon you and for the many harms He has turned away from reaching you, especially for the tremendous favor of Islaam and being granted steadfastness upon it, such that your Islaam has become the most beloved thing to you.

3- Strive to make your heart one which is filled with adoration and glorification of Allaah, the Most Glorified and the Most Exalted, meaning that within yourself this may become the most significant thing you find. It is through joining together in your heart both this love of Allaah, the Most High, and the glorification of Him that will make you steadfast upon His obedience, as someone who properly establishes what He has commanded due to your love of Him, and someone who abandons that which He has forbidden due to your adoration of Him.

4- Strive to be someone upon sincere intention for Allaah the Most Exalted, the Most Magnificent, alone in all of your forms of worship. Furthermore, be someone who trusts and relies upon Him in all of your different situations and conditions, such that you truly implement and actualize the meaning of the verse ❴ *You alone we worship, and You alone we ask for help (for each and everything).* ❵-(Surah al-Fatihah: 5) Strive to bring your heart to a state such that when you have established the commands of Allaah it is done with true submission and surrender, and when you abandon what Allaah has prohibited it is likewise done with true submission and surrender. In this way, you will find that within your worship there is a sweetness and enjoyment, that is not encountered when things are undertaken heedlessly. You will find that in your affairs Allaah assists you and supports you in succeeding, in a way or to a degree that far surpasses what is ever achieved when you simply rely upon yourself.

Secondly, in your relationship with the Messenger of Allaah, may the praise and salutations of Allaah be upon him:

1– That you make your love of him greater than the love of any of the creation, and you place his guidance and Sunnah above the guidance and way of anyone else in creation.

2– That you take him as your leader and model in establishing your acts of worship as well is your general character in life. Such that you remember and keep in mind whenever you are performing an act of worship that you're doing so following his model, and that he is your leader whom you're walking in his footsteps and proceeding carefully upon the path he has established. In the same way in relation to the different aspects of general character the people adopt in life, you strive and put forth effort to adopt his character about which Allaah has said about it, ❰ *And verily, you (O Muhammad) are on an exalted standard of character.* ❱– (Surah al-Qalam: 4) When you adhere and have this focus, you will find that you will be someone with the utmost concern for gaining knowledge of both the Sharee'ah which the Prophet came with as well that of his general character and life.

3– That you stand and proceed as someone who is inviting to the Prophet's Sunnah bringing it victory by defending it, as certainly Allaah, the Most High, will make you successful and grant you victories to the degree that you give victory to the revealed Sharee'ah given to His prophet.

Thirdly, in relation to your daily deeds and undertakings outside of the obligatory matters:

1- For whatever you hope for. As certainly supplication at this time during the night is more likely to be answered. Also recite the statement of Allaah, the Most High ﴾ *Verily! In the creation of the heavens and the earth, and in the alternation of night and day, there are indeed signs for men of understanding.* ﴿ *-(Surah Aal-Imraan: 190)*

2– Pray whatever amount Allaah has written for you to pray in this last part of the night and conclude your optional prayers with a single raka'at of witr as your non-obligatory ritual prayer.

3– Make sure to preserve your engaging in whatever is easy for you from the legislated remembrances which are performed during the morning. Such as saying a hundred times, '*La ilahahila Allaah, la shreeka lahu lahul-mulk wa lahul-hamd wa huwa 'alaa kullee shay'un qadeer*', (which means 'There is none worthy of worship except Allaah alone having no partner with Him. He has the dominion, to Him is due the praise, and He has power and control over everything.')

4- Pray the optional two rakaa'ts of salatul-dhuha ritual prayer

5- Preserve your engaging in whatever is feasible for you from the remembrances which should be performed in the evening each day.

Fourthly, in relation to your preceding upon the path of seeking Sharee'ah knowledge

1– Focus and have true concern about memorizing the Book of Allaah, the Most High. Assign for yourself a specific portion of each day dedicated to reciting the Book of Allaah, and ensure that your recitation be joined with contemplation and understanding its meanings. If during your recitation Allaah blesses you to think of a benefit connected to what you're reciting then stop and take a moment to write that benefit down.

2– Additionally strive to memorize whatever you are able to from the narrations of authentic Sunnah of the Messenger of Allaah, may the praise and salutations of Allaah be upon him, and from scholars' works related to this is working to memorize the collection of hadeeth 'Amdat al-Ahkaam'.

3– Struggle to achieve consistency and well-founded understanding in your studies of Sharee'ah knowledge. Do not simply take from here a single portion of knowledge and from this other area of subject a single benefit or point, since proceeding in that way will both waste your time and scatter your intellectual focus and efforts.

4– Begin with the smaller books and works and focus on them diligently until you are able to gradually progress to those of a higher level above them such that you gain knowledge, step-by-step and by degrees such that it takes firm root within your heart and within yourself you feel satisfied with the progress you've made.

5– Focus and have concern for understanding the fundamental principles behind issues and matters, and be diligent to grasp whatever you encounter from the underlying essentials in foundations. As the well-known saying goes:, "*The one who is cut off from the foundations is deprived of reaching the desired results*".

6- Discuss the different issues studied with your scholar or with someone whom you know has reliable knowledge and practice from your friends and companions, if you have confidence in them being capable of discussing it with you, when you do not find it possible to do so with someone more established and with more knowledge than yourself.

This is what I wished to convey, and I ask Allaah the Most High that he teach you what will benefit you. and benefit you with the knowledge that you learn, that He increase you in knowledge, and grant you the success of being one of His righteous worshipers, and among His successful single party.

Asslaamu aleikum wa rahmatAllaahi wa barakatuhu.

May the praise and salutations of Allaah be upon our Prophet Muhammad, and all praise is due to Allaah Lord of the Worlds.

Written by Muhammad Ibn Saaleh al-'Utheimeen in the month of Rajab in the year 1412

(2)

SIX IMPORTANT ADVICES FOR A SUCCESSFUL LIFE AS A MUSLIM

The first advice: it is necessary for a Muslim that what reached him from the affairs in life would not have missed him, and that what missed him from the affairs in life would not have reached him."

It was narrated that Ibn Dailami said:

"I was confused about this Divine Decree (Qadr), and I was afraid lest that adversely affect my religion and my affairs. So I went to Ubayy bin Ka'b and said: 'O Abu Mundhir! I am confused about the Divine Decree, and I fear for my religion and my affairs, so tell me something about that through which Allaah may benefit me.'

He said: 'If Allaah were to punish the inhabitants of His heavens and of his earth, He would do so and He would not be unjust towards them. And if He were to have mercy on them, His mercy would be better for them than their own deeds. If you had the equivalent of Mount Uhud which you spent in the cause of Allaah, that would not be accepted from you until you believed in the Divine Decree and you know that whatever has befallen you, could not have passed you by; and whatever has passed you by, could not have befallen you; and that if you were to die believing anything other than this, you would enter Hell. And it will not harm you to go to my brother, 'Abdullah bin Mas'ud, and ask him (about this).'

So I went to 'Abdullah and asked him, and he said something similar to what Ubayy had said, and he told me: 'It will not harm you to go to Hudhaifah.' So I went to Hudhaifah and asked him, and he said something similar to what they had said. And he told me: 'Go to Zaid bin Thaabit and ask him.' So I went to Zaid bin Thaabit and asked him, and he said: 'I heard the Messenger of Allaah   say: "If Allaah were to punish the inhabitants of

---

[1]   From the Facebook page of the Sheikh

His heavens and of His earth, he would do so and He would not be unjust towards them. And if He were to have mercy on them, His mercy would be better for them than their own deeds. If you had the equivalent of Mount Uhud which you spent in the cause of Allaah, that would not be accepted from you until you believed in the Divine Decree and you know that whatever has befallen you, could not have passed you by; and whatever has passed you by, could not have befallen you; and that if you were to die believing anything other than this, you would enter Hell" [2]

The second advice: that a Muslim must know that the one who brings benefit or permits harm is only Allaah, the Blessed and the Most High. It is not in the hands of anyone to benefit you with anything, nor in the hands of anyone to harm you with anything except within that which Allaah has already decreed for you. You move and change within the boundaries of Allaah's decree. It is narrated from Ibn 'Abbas, may Allaah be pleased with him, that he said, *{One day, I was riding behind the Prophet, may the praise and salutations of Allaah be upon him, when he said, "O boy! I will instruct you in some matters. Be watchful of Allaah (Commandments of Allaah), He will preserve you. Safeguard His Rights, He will be ever with you. If you ask, ask of Him Alone; and if you need assistance, supplicate to Allaah Alone for help. And remember that if all the people gather to benefit you, they will not be able to benefit you except that which Allaah had foreordained for you; and if all of them gather to do harm to you, they will not be able to afflict you with anything other than that which Allaah had pre-destined against you. The pens had been lifted and the ink has dried}*

---

[2]   Authentic hadeeth narrated in Sunan Ibn Maajah: 77

The third advice: is that a Muslim should have a good suspicion and thoughts about Allaah. As Allaah is the Most Wise, the Most Knowledgeable, the Very Gracious, and the Well-Acquainted with all things. It is narrated from 'Anas Ibn Maalik, may Allaah be pleased with him, that the Messenger of Allaah, may the praise and salutations of Allaah be upon him, said *{The most significant reward is for the greatest of tests. Indeed Allaah when He loves a people He puts them to tests, those who are pleased with it stand as pleased, and the one who is discontent stands as discontent.}*[3]

It is also narrated from Jaabir Ibn 'Abdullaah al-Ansaaree, may Allaah be pleased with him, that he said, I heard the Messenger of Allaah, may Allaah's praise and salutations be upon him, said just three days before his death, *{None of you should die except having good expectation and hoping for good from Allaah, the Most Glorified and the Most Exalted.}*[4]

The fourth advice, is that as a Muslim you should understand that everything that happens to you has some degree of good in it for you, whether you are patient with a difficulties and bad times or you are thankful due to receiving what pleases you and good times.

It is narrated on the authority of Suhaib Ibn Sinan, may Allaah be pleased with him, that the Messenger of Allaah, may Allaah's praise and salutations be upon him, said, {How wonderful is the case of a believer; there is good for him in everything a*nd this applies only to a believer. If prosperity attends him, he expresses gratitude to Allaah and that is good for him; and if adversity befalls him, he endures it patiently and that is better for him.}* [5]

[3]   Authenticated by Sheikh al-Albaanee in his work Silsilaat al-Hadeeth as-Saheehah, vol: 1 pag. 227
[4]   Saheeh Muslims 2877c
[5]   Saheeh Muslim: 27

The fifth advice: it is upon you to be patient, as the life of this world is a place of difficulties and trials, starting from the beginning of your life until you die. Allaah, the Blessed and the Most High, ❖ *Who has created death and life, that He may test you which of you is best in deed. And He is the All-Mighty, the Oft-Forgiving;* ❖-(Surah al-Mulk: 2)

From the different types of difficulties which are tests are what was mentioned by Allaah the Blessed and the Most High, ❖ *And certainly, We shall test you with something of fear, hunger, loss of wealth, lives and fruits, but give glad tidings to as-saabirin (the patient ones, etc.).* ❖-(Surah al-Baqarah: 155)

Here Allaah describes the nature of difficulties, and He offers the solution to them, which is patience. The ruling on having patience varies, in some circumstances it is something which is an obligation upon you, and in others is something recommended. Being patient with having to perform acts of obedience to Allaah is itself obligatory. Whereas being patient with having to perform acts of obedience to Allaah that are themselves recommended, is itself something only recommended. Similarly, being patient in the obligation of turning away from forbidden matters, is itself obligatory. Whereas, being patient in the turning away from detested or disliked matters, itself carries the ruling of being recommended. Thus being patient regarding whatever Allaah has decreed for you of difficulties that you are tested with as a Muslim is an obligatory type of patience.

The sixth advice: That you look and consider the state of those who are below you in matters, this is the most suitable to prevent you from dismissing and making light of the blessings of Allaah upon you. It is narrated from Abu Hurairah, may Allaah be pleased with him, that the Messenger of Allaah, may the praise and salutations of Allaah be upon him, said, *{When one of you looks at* *someone who is superior to him in property and appearance, he should then look at someone who is inferior to him}*[6]

The narration in Saheeh Muslim states, *{Look at those who are inferior to you and do not look at those who are superior to you, for this will keep you from belittling Allaah's favor to you.}* All praise is due to Allaah, who through His blessing we have completed this act of righteousness.

May the praise and salutations of Allaah be upon the Prophet Muhammad, upon his family, and his Companions, along with him blessing you with continuing health and well being.

---

[6] Found in both of two most authentic hadeeth collections, Saheeh al-Bukharee and Saheeh Muslim, with the same text and narrator.

(3)

HOW DO WE DETERMINE WHAT IS
THE TRUTH OF A MATTER?

(Consider the situation where:) I believe that the one who opposes me in some matter stands upon a position of falsehood! And the one who differs with me sees himself as the one on the truth and that I am upon falsehood! And perhaps you, a third person, hold that both of our positions are incorrect and that your position is actually what is the truth! So who among us is upon the truth?

In order for us to correctly ascertain which of us is upon the truth we must follow specific steps:[1]

Firstly from what we affirm within our religion is: there should be no issuing of blame or censure against the one upon the Sunnah who takes an opposing position when that religious difference of positions based upon valid scholastic efforts to independently determine the correct position. This is whenever there is no clear Sharee'ah evidence that would require both sides to accept and adhere to it. Rather, in such cases there should be advising between them both without blame! In the situation of this first type of difference it is required that I verify the soundness of my own position in relation to the one who differs with me. It might be that I state to myself: What I hold is correct but there is a possibility that it may be incorrect, and what he states is incorrect but there is a possibility it may be correct!

Yet, if the differing is of a second type meaning it is the case where there is indeed clear Sharee'ah evidence that I am affirming and following which does require both sides to adhere to that evidence, then this situation is properly established in my statement: "I am upon the truth and the one who differs with me is upon that which is incorrect and wrong". As such I should censure him for this position which is incorrect, meaning opposing the

___
[1]   This is posts joined together from several separate posts in a series by the Sheikh

111

clear evidence, while explaining to him what is correct and sound in this issue, and clarifying the Sharee'ah evidences which are required being accepted and followed.

I should clarify his mistaken position and what he falsely believes and clings to of what is actually an error! As it is an obligation upon us to implement what Allaah has commanded us all to do, ❦ *O you who have believed, obey Allah and obey the Messenger and those in authority among you. And if you disagree over anything, refer it to Allah and the Messenger, if you should believe in Allah and the Last Day. That is the best way and best in result.* ❦ – (Surah an-Nisaa': 59) Yet the people who generally follow their desires wrongly attempt to classify every difference as only the first mentioned type, where there is no censure or blame, due to lack of clear definite evidence. Yet some of the newcomers or beginners in knowledge wrongly, do the opposite, and make every disagreement and differing of the second type in which there is only one acceptable position, because of definite evidence!

For this reason, it is said in summary that you can come to know that you stand upon the truth by means of one of three clear indicators.

Firstly, by retuning back to the source texts of the Qur'aan and Sunnah

Secondly: Looking and comparing to whatever the Prophet and his Companions were upon (as they are the Jamaa'ah) and

Thirdly, returning and referring to the people of knowledge who are available to you.

THE FIRST INDICATOR

The second step which enables you to distinguish what is the truth in religious matters is that Allaah, the Blessed and the Most High, has said ❦ *O you who have believed, obey Allah and obey the Messenger and those in authority among you. And if you disagree over anything, refer it to Allah and the Messenger, if you should believe in Allah and the Last Day. That is the best way and best in result.*❩–(Surah an-Nisaa': 59)

This is the first indicator we use from the correct indications of determining the truth when there are differences. By this meaning that we refer our differences back to Allaah and his Messenger. Referring it back to Allaah means referring it back to His Word that He sent down. And referring it back to his Messenger, means referring it back to his Sunnah

But whenever the specific nature of the issue is one which prevents the people from referring back to the Qur'aan and Sunnah and understanding the matter from them directly, then the Messenger of Allaah, may the praise and salutations of Allaah be upon him, guided us to an additional way by which we implement this command to refer every matter back to Allaah and his Messenger, may Allaah's praise and salutations be upon him. This additional way is the second indicator in determining the truth.

THE SECOND INDICATOR

The second indicator towards understanding what is the truth of the matter, is to weigh and contrast whatever it is that we have and compare it to whatever the Messenger of Allaah, may the praise and salutations of Allaah be upon him, and his Companions stood upon in relation to it. This was what he guided the Muslims to, may Allaah's praise and salutations be upon him, when differing, differences, and splitting occurred among the Muslims. The hadeeth related to this command is narrated in Sunan Abu Dawood narration number 4597. It is been declared as having an acceptable level of authenticity by Hafidh Ibn Hajar and Sheikh al-Albaanee in his verification of the narrations found in Sunan Abu Dawood.

It was narrated on the authority of Mu'aweeyah Ibn Abu Sufyaan, may Allaah be pleased with him, that he stood among the people and said, the Messenger of Allaah stood among us and said,

{Certainly there were those from the people who were sent revealed scripture who split and separated into seventy-two sects. This Ummah, of mine, will split into seventy three sects, seventy two of which will be punished in Hellfire, and one of which will be in Jannah, they are the Jamaa'ah, those Muslim who remained united upon my guidance.}

In a related similar narration it states,

{There will come forth from my Ummah those whom their false desires will dominate and run through them as the disease of rabies runs through a dog. There is not a vein nor a joint of the body except that these desires will enter into it among them.}

The term Jamaa'ah in the first narration is explained by a narration transmitted by at-Tirmidhee no: 2641. It was narrated by 'Abdullah Ibn 'Amr, that the Messenger of Allaah, may the praise and salutations of Allaah be upon him, said,

{This Ummah will be confronted with those same trials which confronted Bani Isra'eel, step by step, to such a degree that if there was a man from the previous nation who would approach his mother to have sexual relations openly, then there will be from my Ummah someone to follow that same misguidance.

Indeed Bani Isra'eel separated into seventy-two different sects. And this Ummah of mine, will split into seventy three sects, all of which will be punished in Hellfire, except for one.". "So it was asked of him, "Who are those from that one, oh Messenger of Allaah?" He replied, " Those who are upon what I and my Companions are upon."} at-Tirmidhee stated, "This narration has an uncommon specification which we do not know of any text similar to it, except what is found through this specific report and transmission."

It contains a narrator al-Afreeqee who is weak, but it is supported by other related narrations to be assessed as authentic.

The meaning of these narrations is that we comprehend and recognize the truth by looking to the Jamaa'ah, that being those Muslims who stand upon what the Messenger of Allaah, may Allaah's praise and salutations be him, was upon. Therefore regarding any and every matter we investigate what exactly the Messenger and his Companions stood upon, or what is similar to this from their guidance. Then we hold firmly to that as certainly that is the ◈*believers way*◈.

THE THIRD INDICATOR

The third signpost which enables you to distinguish what is the truth in religious matters: turning and referring to the scholars of Islaam. Just as is mentioned in Surah an-Nahl: 43 ◈*...So ask the people of the message if you do not know.* ◈ And this is whenever it is not easy or beyond your capacity to refer directly to the Qur'aan and Sunnah in order to derive guidance connected to the issue in which there are differences, in order to discern what is the position of truth in that matter.

Similarly, this is necessary whenever it is not easy or beyond your capacity to look directly to what the Messenger of Allaah, may Allaah's praise and salutations be him, and his Companions were upon. The signpost is implemented or realized by turning to the scholars and asking them directly. It is for this reason that knowledge is lost among a people by their losing their scholars as they die.

Finally, it is mentioned that the matter of differing with others has etiquettes that should be followed, just as it has a proper way of management and proceeding. And the success is with Allaah.

(4)

THERE ARE TWO CATEGORIES OF
TRUE KNOWLEDGE

bn Taymeeyah, may Allaah have mercy upon them both, in his work explaining the fundamentals of commentary upon the Book of Allaah stated,

"Indeed the books people have compiled and written as explanations of the Qur'aan are filled with both that which is inadequate and deficient as well is that which is rich and nourishing. They contain both statements which are clear falsehood along with those which are undisputably the truth.

That which is knowledge is either what has been transmitted by those Muslims who are reliable from the one infallible person who was sent to humanity, or is statement which is based upon a valid Sharee'ah evidence.

Whatever is not found to be one of these two, is either a clear falsehood which is rejected, or that which we withhold from due to not having clear assessment as to whether it is counterfeit and so worthless or if it is something not actually criticized."

Sheikh Muhammad Ibn Saaleh al-'Utheimeen, may Allaah have mercy upon, him in his commentary of this work of Ibn Taymeeyah, explain this saying,

"That which is (truly) knowledge is either what has been transmitted by those Muslims who are reliable from the one infallible person who was sent to humanity" This is the Messenger of Allaah, may the praise and salutations of Allaah be upon him, and the second category is that statement which has its basis upon known evidence in Islaam. By this meaning a statement from some of the Companions of the Messenger of Allaah, or from their Successors, or those with knowledge who came after them. But such statements

must be based upon a known accepted evidence whether that is an intellectual conclusion within the framework of the Sharee'ah or a directly transmitted statement of knowledge.

It is from this that we affirm the position of the evidence, derived by valid analogy, and it is considered a form of evidence based upon an intellectual conclusion. This general understanding is something that is necessary that we make a principal in properly understanding what is truly knowledge, because knowledge is either what is reliably transmitted from the infallible messenger who was sent, or it is a statement of knowledge that has a clear basis in a valid evidence.

He stated, **"Whatever is not found to be one of these two, is either a clear falsehood which is rejected, or that which we withhold from due to not having clear assessment as to whether it is counterfeit and so worthless or if it is something not actually criticized.** "

This statement is made in a manner of speech that rhymes. Rhyming speech, if it is not done in a way which is theatrical and artificial, then there is no doubt that it beautifies a person's statements, and fosters someone's attraction to what is said. These rhyming statements occasionally are found in the speech of the Messenger of Allaah, may the praise and salutations of Allaah be upon him, but without any theatrics or artificialness.

The author of the work continues to say, **"Whatever is not found to be one of these two..."**

He indicates these two clear categories: that knowledge which is transmitted reliably from the infallible prophet, and that statement of knowledge which is based upon valid evidences.

*He stated, "...***is either a clear falsehood which is rejected,***" this means in comparison to that which is transmitted reliably from the Prophet.*

Concluding he states, **"or that which we withhold from due to not having clear knowledge as to whether it is counterfeit and so worthless or that which is not actually criticized."** *meaning that which we withhold from either definitively accepting or rejecting. Based upon this we say that they are three categories:*

That statement which we know is authentic and sound knowledge, it being the first category.

That statement which we know is falsehood or incorrect, with that being the second category.

And lastly that which it is obligatory that we withhold from either accepting or rejecting and this is the third category.

This last category is that which we do not know whether it is from what is been transmitted reliably from the infallible messenger, or secondly whether it is a statement which is actually based upon known and accepted evidence or opposing this that which is obvious falsehood which we must reject. In this last case we don't know whether it is this category or that, because the first category of statements is accepted, whereas the second category of statements is rejected, and the third category we withhold from."

Sheikh Saaleh ibn 'Abdul-'Azeez Aal-Sheikh, may Allaah preserve him, stated in his own commentary of the same work,

"It is been mentioned to you from what we heard in this work that what is truly knowledge is of two categories, without there being any third category. Firstly, it is that knowledge which has been transmitted, from that individual who is free from making any mistake in relation to the religion. This encompasses the Book of Allaah, the Sunnah, and the Consensus of the Muslim Ummah based upon these, because both the Qur'aan and

the Sunnah are revelation from Allaah, the Most High. Furthermore, verified Consensus is considered infallible from mistakes, because what has been mentioned in a number of authentic narrations, which all support each other, that the Prophet, may the praise and salutations of Allaah be upon him, clarified and explained that the Muslim Ummah will never unite in consensus upon what is falsehood. Therefore the proofs which are considered infallible in Islaam are the Qur'aan or the Book of Allaah, the Sunnah, and the Consensus of the Muslim Ummah.

His statement, "**or is statement which is based upon a valid Sharee'ah evidence.**" *Initially it was explained that knowledge is that which is transmitted from the infallible prophet. Here the discussion is concerning those independently derived conclusions, from one of the scholars suitable and capable to undertake that scholastic task, conclusions which are based upon a known valid evidence. This description excludes matters which are wrongly or incorrectly considered evidence. This is because some of the people who have extremism towards their scholars' statements without mentioned evidence say, [But the scholar must have had evidence in this issue, meaning the issue which we are holding to, even though he did not mention it to us.] Yet for us, our way is to worship Allaah according to that which is clearly indicated of valid Sharee'ah evidences, since this is what is truly considered knowledge.*

The scholar Ibn 'Abdul-Bar, may Allaah the Most High, have mercy upon him, stated explicitly in his well-known work 'al-Jamee'a' that the scholars of Islaam stand in consensus, that anyone who blindly follows another, is not considered a scholar in Islaam himself. The individual who is considered a scholar, is the one who holds or makes his statements based upon and valid stated Sharee'ah evidence. Knowledge is that statement which is based upon valid evidence, or based upon what is reliably transmitted from the infallible prophet of Allaah.

A statement which is based upon valid evidence can mean that a scholar makes an independently derived scholastic conclusion or ruling but that statement must have evidence behind it. By this meaning that he directly speaks and mentions his evidence or that his statement is the result of or indirectly comes from valid evidence. This is what we benefit from in the books explaining the meanings of the Qur'aan. Either their explanations of the scholar explaining the Qur'aan has a clear stated evidence, or his statement is based upon evidence which is well-known to the scholars.

Such that, for example, they state, "The evidence of Ibn 'Abbass is such and such." or they say "the evidence of 'Alee in his explanation of this verse is such and such."

...Lastly there is the third category. It is that statement which is not from what has been transmitted from our infallible prophet, nor is it is statement whose foundation is a valid evidence. This last category is not considered to truly be from knowledge, it is that which is not acted upon but stands as that is withheld from, as was mentioned. It is that statement which it is not known to be what clearly rejects guidance or something counterfeit, meaning that we cannot discern whether it is authentic or not. (Perhaps) it is someone's statement without stated evidence, and we do not know any evidence supporting it. But it addition, on the other side, there is no apparent evidence which indicates that the statement is something clearly false, then we simply attribute it to the one who stated it without relying upon it for guidance. This understanding is crucial in regard to what will come, if Allaah the Most High so wills, in studying this work about the guidelines of explaining the Qur'aan."

Sheikh Muqbil also discussed the importance of understanding the distinction between the position of Salaf upon evidences and the position of an individual scholar from among them, as this is directly related to the understanding of the essential sources of the religion of the Qur'aan and Sunnah. Sheikh Muqbil was asked, [1]

"Is there a difference between the understanding of the Salaf and the understanding of one individual from the Salaf- of a specific source text, and between a scholars' statement without direct evidence?"

Sheikh Muqbil asks, "Between the understanding of the Salaf and the understanding of one individual from them?"

Questioner: **"About an evidence from the source texts."**

Sheikh Muqbil, replies, "Yes, there is a difference."

Questioner, **"And between the general understanding of the Salaf and a specific scholars' opinion without direct evidence?"**

Sheikh Muqbil, says, "As for a scholars' opinion without direct evidence it is not considered a fundamental proof in the religion. As Allaah says, **❴ Follow what has been sent down unto you from your Lord (the Qur'aan and Prophet Muhammad's Sunnah), and follow not any Auliyaa' (protectors and helpers, etc. who order you to associate partners in worship with Allaah), besides Him (Allaah). Little do you remember! ❵** *-(Surah al-A'raf: 3)*

Lastly, Sheikh Saaleh Ibn Fauzaan, may Allaah preserve him, said,[2]

"It is not permissible to adopt the statement of a scholar of Islamic jurisprudence, no matter how extensive his level of understanding and knowledge, except upon having confidence that his position is based upon some authentic evidence."

---

[1] From ruling no. 4639 from muqbel.net
[2] Explanation of the Structured Poem al-Ha'eeyah: pg. 63

(5)

DO NOT CONNECT THE TRUTH OF ISLAAM TO INDIVIDUALS

heikh al-'Utheimeen, may Allaah have mercy upon him, illustrated the meaning of following the Prophet in this which Sheikh Ibn Baaz has mentioned in Day 16, may Allaah have abundant mercy upon them both. As recorded in an audio tape with his voice, during a public gathering, he said,

"**This person has requested to read a poem, should we permit him to do that? Yes?..Good.**"

The young person begins reading saying, "In the name of Allaah, the Most gracious the Most Merciful. All praise is due to Allaah, may praise and salutation be upon the Messenger of Allaah. To proceed, esteemed sheikh I ask for your permission to proceed with the poem."

Sheikh al-'Utheimeen, "**Yes, please proceed...**"

The young poet begins,

" *Oh My Ummah this night will be followed,*

by a dawn whose rays of light will spread forth upon the land.

Goodness will go forward extend, with victory is expected.

The truth will spread regardless of the working of evil.

This is through a revival of following guidance that Allaah has blessed us with,

proceeding upon purity, without hindrances nor barriers.

As long as there stands among us the son of Saaleh, As long as there stands among us the son of Saaleh, the sheikh of our revival.

Since with the presence of the likes of him we have hope for our success and being triumphant."

Sheikh al-'Utheimeen interrupts here and stops the poet saying, "**I do not approve of this section of the poem. No, I do not agree with this line as I do not want the truth of Islaam to be connected to individuals.**

125

Everyone will eventually die, and if we connect the truth to individuals. Then if this person dies, the people are weakened in what they hope for. Therefore I say that if you can, simply change this section to 'As long as the Book of Allah and the Sunnah of His messenger remain among us.' That this would be good."

The poet then says, "*As long as the Book of Allah and the Sunnah of His messenger remain among us.*"

Hearing this Sheikh al-'Utheimeen approves, saying, "*Yes.*"

But the young poet then adds "*...and Ibn al-'Utheimeen*"

Sheikh al-'Utheimeen again interrupts the young man here saying,

"**No, this is not correct.**" Some speak to him and there is discussion quietly for a moment with the people. The young poet begins again then changes the words and so says, "*...and our scholar*"

However Sheikh al-'Utheimeen again interrupts the young man, saying, "**No, no...**" Others there then ask the sheikh to allow the young man to continue but he refuses saying "**No, no,...no I do not approve of this. If this is what you have to present, then simply bring forth a question.**" But others ask him to allow it to be read. They again try to convince hm. "**Yes?...**" He listened to their reasoning, " and then said, "*.... never what is wrong with you...*" He then says to all those present,

"**I advise you now and from this point onwards, to not attach and connect the truth to individuals. As people can always stray away the truth, such that Ibn Mas'ood said, '*Whoever wishes to follow someone in righteousness then follow one who has died, and the living person is never safe from being put to trial.*" An individual, if you connect the truth to him, may feel pride in himself, and we seek refuge in Allaah from that, and of turning to a path which is not correct. It is for this reason that I advise you all now, do not make the truth something that is connected to individuals.

Firstly, a person is never, and I ask Allaah for safety for you and us, is never safe from deviating or falling to a trial.

Secondly, every single person must die and no one will always remain alive. (Allaah has said) ❧ *And We granted not to any human being immortality before you (O Muhammad); then if you die, would they live forever?*❧ – (Surah al-Anbiyyah: 34).

Thirdly, every son of Aadam is only human, he might feel false pride if he sees the people praising, honoring him, and gathering around him, such that he might be afflicted with this. Then he may start to believe he is free from making mistakes, presume some infallibility for himself, coming to believe that every matter he states is upon the truth, and that every way he chooses to proceed upon is something legislated. In that he would reach the point of self-ruin and his own destruction.

Due to this, once when one man praised another in the presence of the Messenger of Allaah, may the praise and salutations of Allaah be upon him, the Prophet, may the praise and salutations of Allaah be upon him, said to him, {…You have cut the neck of your companion.} or he said, {You have broken the back of your companion..}

So I thank our brother, even without having heard what the poem contains, due to what he had wished to say about me, and for the good feeling he has towards me. I ask Allah to make me like this good suspicion that brother holds of me and increase me in such good, but I do not like that this is said. And I ask Allaah to reward you with a good reward from Him the Most High, and I ask Him to both bless you with good and reward you, yes"

(6)

PRINCIPLES & CHARACTERISTICS OF THE WAY OF THE FIRST GENERATIONS

1. From among these principles and characteristics of those upon this way of the first generations of Muslims is that they invite the Muslim men and women to respond to the invitation of their Lord the Master of the Clear Truth, and the call of their prophet who was the trustworthy adviser, by them making a truthful sincere return to fully following the guidance of the Noble Book of Allaah and that of the pure Sunnah in every area of their lives and affairs. They invite them to undertake this upon the methodology of the righteous predecessors of this Ummah, and upon the believing way of all those Muslims who followed them in goodness from the cultivating scholars and the pious close associates of Allaah firmly. As they are the people who adhered to His guidance, acted upon it, and called the general people to it with merciful conduct, while standing on straightforward guidance, both hoping for the mercy of Allaah and fearing His punishment.

2. From among these principles and characteristics of those upon this way of the first generations of Muslims is that they diligently focus upon knowledge of the truth from its fundamental sources which have reached them from the earlier age of the Ummah, then spread it to the people of the earth standing upon the truth, mercifully bringing them the truth while bringing forth an evident presentation of the objective His guidance, establishing the proofs in front of Allaah and humanity.

3. From among these principles and characteristics of those upon this way of the first generations of Muslims is that they establish the obligation of offering sound advice to those requiring it from among the Muslim men and women, as this is one of the most significant obligations

PRINCIPLES

---

[1] Taken from Al-Ajweebah as-Sadeedah Alaa al-'Asilah ar-Rasheedah under the original section heading -From The Well Established Principles & Enduring Excellent Distinct Characteristics' of the Way of the Call of the Salaf

and purist forms of gaining closeness to Allaah. This is done upon the condition that the one offering the advice is distinguished by knowledge, forbearance, truthfulness and sincere intention. How else could they possibly be properly standing in the honorable position of offering advice and counsel? Indeed the noble Prophet, may the praise and salutations of Allaah be upon him, said, *{The religion is the sincere offering of advice...}*

4. From among their principles and characteristics of the righteous predecessors of the Ummah and those who walk in their footsteps in every age is that their methodology, is not something limited only to the area of beliefs. Rather it is both beliefs and actions. In affirming this carrying the meaning of actions to convey what is properly intended by the term. Therefore "Salafeeyah" is beliefs and actions.

5. From among these principles and characteristics of those upon this way of the first generations of Muslims is that they consistently strive and always put forth sincere struggling to unite the Muslims and establish proper cooperation between them upon the basis of goodness and the fear of Allaah. Certainly there is a distinctive good achieved through uniting the Muslims in a single rank, and actualizing the way of truly cooperating upon goodness and the fear of Allaah. It is only accomplished by the adherence to the Sunnah, reviving it, spreading it, while at the same time fighting against innovations in the religion, since through these false innovations in the religion the people of innovation intend to replace the practices of the authentic Sunnah and realize their flawed objectives, whether they do so upon a good intention or a wicked negative one.

6- From among these principles and characteristics of those upon this way of the first generations of Muslims is that when disputes and controversies occur they refer back to the Book of Allaah and the Sunnah to seek guidance. This is something required by and directed to by both the noble revelation and sound intellectual consideration just as Allaah, the Noble Supporter of the believers says, *❖ ...if you differ in anything amongst yourselves, refer it to Allaah and His Messenger, if you believe in Allaah and in the Last Day. That is better and more suitable for final determination.❖*-(Surah an-Nisa': 59) Without any argument this is the only correct criterion for resolving religious disputes with justice and fairness, meaning that these two sources be taken as the final scale as understood by the first generations upon sound principles and strong fundamentals. This Muslim Ummah places the criterion of what determines its overall well being and success upon what was found with its early ages and generation. For this reason they must always return to the source texts of the Qur'aan and Sunnah, as comprehended by the precise steadfast scholars, those who, with exemplary character, are the righteous close associates of Allaah.

7. From among these principles and characteristics is that the methodology of tasfeeyah -or clarification of what is truly Islaam, and tarbeeyah -or education and cultivation- is clearly affirmed and established as a true and correct perspective coming from the first three generations of Islaam, and is something well known to the people of merit from among them, as must be concluded by considering all the related evidence. What is intended by tasfeeyah, when referring to it generally, is clarifying that which is the truth from that which is falsehood, what is goodness from that which is harmful and corrupt, and when referring to its specific meanings, it is distinguishing the noble Sunnah of the Prophet and the people of the Sunnah from those innovated matters

brought into the religion by the people who are supporters of such innovations. As for what is intended by tarbeeyah, it is calling all of the creation to adopt and take on the manners and embrace the excellent character invited to by that guidance revealed to them by their Lord through His worshiper and Messenger Muhammad, may Allaah's praise and salutations be upon him. This is in order that that they might have truly good character, manners, and behavior. As without this they cannot have a good life, put right their present condition, or work towards a successful final destination. And we seek refuge in Allaah from the evil of not being able to achieve that rectification."

8. From among these principles and characteristics of those upon this way of the first generations of Muslims is that they adhere firmly, inwardly and outwardly to obeying the Muslim rulers in what is acceptable and supplicate for them both openly and in secret. They ask Allaah that these rulers be guided, assisted, and directed towards what would make them successful by Allaah. This is since their rectification, that of the Muslim rulers, is a cause for the rectification of the general worshipers and the lands of the Muslims, as well as the opposite situation- of their corruption- except when Allaah in His mercy decrees this not be the case. What is considered as being from the legitimate obedience to them is:

a. Properly establishing their rights, encouraging the citizens' hearts to be favorable towards them, as an act of obedience to Allaah and implementing the guidance of the Messenger of Allaah, may Allaah's praise and salutations be upon him.

b. Rejecting and turning away from revolting against them through any of the minor or major ways that this is done, whether that be by armed revolt or agitating speech that inflames and agitates the common people.

The source texts of the Qur'aan and Sunnah prohibit this revolting against them due to what it causes of harm to the state of the peoples' religion, just as it causes the corrupting of the Muslims' honor and the spilling of their blood, and the loss of their overall general state of well being. Generally, it causes chaos to spread among the Muslims, and plants the seeds of the hostility within their societies similar to that found before the emergence of Islaam. This is along with other clear harms resulting from both statements and actions that our Sharee'ah does not approve of, nor does any individual of sound intelligence.

9. From among these principles and characteristics of those upon this way of the first generations of Muslims is that they have a definitive conviction and faith that this call of guidance and light takes its strength and derives its illumination and light from the authenticity of the divine proofs. Those proofs came down through revelation given to the one sent to distinguish between the truth and falsehood, meaning the Prophet, may the praise and salutations of Allaah be upon him. Furthermore, the strength of this call is not taken from numerous statements made by men and their varied opinions, nor is it harmed or lessened in any way due to the small number of people truly walking upon its path of clear truth, nor are those upon it deceived by the numerous groups and sects that deviate away from the original guidance of the leader and seal of the prophets and messengers, may the best of praise and the highest of mention of those in the heavens be upon him.

10. From among these principles and characteristics of those upon this way of the first generations of Muslims is that they earnestly love the noble Companions of the Messenger of Allaah and cling to following them in all the levels of Islaam, emaan, and Ihsaan. They view this as an obligation from the obligations of Islaam. The truth is that anyone who curses the Companions of the Messenger of Allaah, abuses them, reviles or criticizes one of them, whether he shows open hatred towards them or conceals it, has gathered together the transgressions of apostasy, major sins, and lesser sins. Indeed, anyone who opposes those who are the close associates of Allaah by reviling them, cursing, showing enmity, and expressing hatred towards them is indeed opposing Allaah. Look at the punishment of Allaah which He previously sent down upon such people, upon corruption and crimes against Him, which they were not able to be push or turn away.

The acknowledged evidences of this oh noble reader is from the established proofs within the religion of Islaam. One of them is the statement of the Lord of Might and Majesty in describing His prophet Muhammad, may the praise and salutations of Allaah be upon him, and describing his noble Companions, ❖ *Muhammad is the Messenger of Allaah, and those who are with him are severe against disbelievers, and merciful among themselves. You see them bowing and falling down prostrate (in prayer), seeking Bounty from Allaah and His Good Pleasure. The mark of them (i.e. of their Faith) is on their faces (foreheads) from the traces of (their) prostration during prayers. This is their description in the Tauraat. But their description in the Injeel is like a sown seed which sends forth its shoot, then makes it strong, it then becomes thick, and it stands straight on its stem, delighting the sowers that He may enrage the disbelievers with them. Allaah has promised those among them who believe (i.e. all those who follow Islamic Monotheism, the religion of Prophet Muhammad till the Day of Resurrection) and do righteous good deeds, forgiveness and a mighty reward (Paradise).*≫-(Surah al-Fath: 29) Their state, the one with enmity towards the Companions, is that which His chosen Messenger informed us about from Allaah, *{...I will declare war against him who treats with hostility a pious worshipper of Mine...}* [2]

11. From among these principles and characteristics of those upon this way of the first generations of Muslims is that they focus and give attention to rectifying the hearts and minds of the worshippers from the diseases of misconceptions and doubts which Shaytaan directs towards them in his efforts to strike at their emaan and faith. Similarly, they also focus and give attention to rectifying the hearts and souls the worshippers from the diseases of desires and urges which Shaytaan inflames and incites within them in order to also strike at their emaan and faith from that second direction. Defending against these two diseases requires two things: the first of them is patience, and the second is certainty just as Allaah has said, ≪ *And We made from among them (Children of Israel), leaders, giving guidance under Our Command, when they were patient and used to believe with certainty in Our Ayaat (proofs, evidences, verses, lessons, signs, revelations, etc.).* ≫-(Surah as-Sajdah: 24) Indeed, Allaah the Most High informs humanity through these noble verses that leadership in the religion in gained through having sufficient patience and sufficient certainty. Indeed it is patience which defends against and steers away from desires and urges unlawfully turned towards, and it is certainty of faith that defends against and turns away from us misconceptions and doubts in the religion.

12. From among these principles and characteristics of those upon this way of the first generations of Muslims is that they hold that the later part and state of the Muslim Ummah will not be rectified and made sound and healthy except by that matter and remedy which rectified the first

---

[2] Saheeh al-Bukhaaree: 386

part and age of the Muslim Ummah. This magnificent principle which was held by the first generations and those who followed their believer's way throughout history is supported and born witness to by the source texts of the Qur'aan and Sunnah which indicate this principle, which is clearly understood by those understanding the texts' correct meanings.

13. From among these principles and characteristics of those upon this way of the first generations of Muslims is that they have reverence and respect for the guiding cultivating scholars of the Ummah, both living and those who have died. They have true love for them and take knowledge from those among them who are alive and study and learn from the books of knowledge from those among them who have died. Their defense of the scholars generally is one of the hallmarks which is a distinguishing feature of the methodology of the first generations of Islaam, just as the opposite, the lack or failure to do so, is a hallmark of other false methodologies. The general practice of wrongly attacking the scholars and labeling them with negative labels and nicknames, charging them with false accusations, and various claimed faults is a distinct characteristic of the people of innovation and misguidance, whom Shaytaan has deceived and made their evil actions appealing to them.

14. From among these principles and characteristics of those upon this way of the first generations of Muslims is that they are pleased with the coming to guidance of someone who accepts the guidance of the Sharee'ah, and they are saddened by the one who chooses to remain seduced and deceived by misguidance- without their being displeased with Allaah's decree. This is a clear characteristic of the first generations of Muslims and those who followed in their footsteps, striving to adopt the excellent character which they had.

15. From among these principles and characteristics of those upon this way of the first generations of Muslims is that they build their bonds of love upon the guidance of the Sharee'ah, and direct it towards those upon the Sunnah, in this way implementing the methodology of allegiance and disassociation which is from the clear principles of the Methodology of the Salaf. No one shares this characteristic except those committed to their way and who hold themselves to their way of behavior.

16. From among these principles and characteristics of those upon this way of the first generations of Muslims is that they hold, as something which has brilliant clarity being transmitted from the first generations of the Ummah and those who followed them throughout time, that it is firm reality of those seeking of knowledge in every age and time, that they have a strong need to have understanding of the books of refutations written against those people who follow their desires in the religion and innovate within it. This also applies to knowing the books of criticism and commendation of individuals in the religion. This is so they are able to both warn against the deceptions of those who have been rightly criticized for following their desires, and be protected from the evil and harm of those changing and innovating in the religion. Furthermore they are those who have diligence is establishing the correct sounds beliefs of Islaam, and established efforts defending the clear authentic Sunnah from those who wish to attack it.

17- From among these principles and characteristics of those upon this way of the first generations of Muslims is that they are those who know, act upon, and teach others to directly supplicate and call up our Lord alone who is the Master of all the Heavens.

18. From among these principles and characteristics of those upon this way of the first generations of Muslims is that they hold that the truth is what is established guidance that stands between to the two ways of misguidance of negligence and extremism.

19. From among these principles and characteristics of those upon this way of the first generations of Muslims is that they are the people of the people of the Sunnah and adherence to the Jamaa'ah. They stand in a middle position between the extremism of the sect of the Khawaarij who declare Muslims as disbelievers for committing major sins, and the extremism of the sect of the Murji'ah who state that the commission of major sins does not affect a worshipers' emaan or faith at all, in the same way that it is established that someone upon disbelief is not helped by acts of obedience. The specific meaning of the middle path and balance of the people of the Sunnah between these two misguided sects in this issue, is that they state upon evidences that the Muslim who commits a major sin becomes a transgressor due to his sin, yet he remains a believer due to what remains within him of reduced emaan or faith. They state upon evidence that the Muslim who died while persistently committing a major sin, dies as a Muslim under the threat of Allaah's punishment. If Allah so wills, He may punish him in Hellfire to the degree of that worshipper's transgression. Or if He so wills, He may forgive him and enter the worshipper into Paradise without that person having to suffer anything of the punishment due of Hellfire.

20. Establishing and fulfilling the need to scholastically refute those who have opposed the guidance of Islaam is from among these principles and characteristics of those upon this way of the first generations of Muslims. This is specifically true in terms of those misguided people who attribute themselves to Islaam yet stand upon and call to innovation in the religion. Just as was mentioned

by Ibn al-Qayyim in Madaarij as-Saalikeen[3], where he stated, "*There is a severe condemnation from the first three generations of Muslims and the leading scholars who adhered to their way, of innovation in the religion, calling out to distinguish the people upon that in the various lands of the earth, and warning away from the trial they bring to the religion with the most serious of warnings. We find this conveyed from them with an intensity not found in relation to their warnings about transgressions of immorality, general injustice, and offensive acts against Islaam. This was because the harm of innovation in the religion is much more significant, it conflicts with, and damage to the religion is greater.*"

I say: because of the serious harm it causes, meaning innovation, the undertaking of refutation of the people involved in innovation is from the greatest doors of jihaad in Allaah's path, has a significant place in struggling against innovation, and stands as the best form of striving in the path of Allaah to defend Islaam. Ibn Taymeeyah, may Allaah have mercy upon him, said, (Majmu'a al-Fataawa vol. 4 pg. 13) "The one who refutes the people of innovation is someone striving in Allaah's path, so much so that Yahya Ibn Yahya said: Defending the Sunnah is the best form of jihaad in the path of Allaah..."

As to how this refutation is carried out, it may be through debating and having dialogs with them and others using the revealed source texts, explaining aspects of what the texts indicate to clarify issues, dispel misconceptions, and remove the harm that they cause the general people. This is especially true since a number of them attribute themselves to being from the people of knowledge. For this reason such efforts are considered jihaad in the path of Allaah.

PRINCIPLES

---

[3]   Madaarij as-Saalikeen, vol. 1 pg. 372

21. Those who follow this methodology of the Salaf hold that every effort of calling to the people to Islaam, done in the name of Islaam and the Sharee'ah which was revealed to the best of creation, but is not specifically established upon the authentic way and methodology of the final Prophet, will not be accepted by Allaah, nor will it bear the fruits of true success. This is because such calls are divorced and separated from the real causes of true results and success for the Muslims, regardless of how well organized their efforts are and frequently circulated it is within Muslim societies.

22. From among these principles and characteristics of those upon this way of the first generations of Muslims is carefully selecting and choosing the teacher you study with and the book that you study from. You see that they choose to place within their personal libraries the books of the scholars of the first three generations of Islaam and those of the people of knowledge who follow in their way, due to these people being free from both deviations of belief and methodology. Similarly, they chose the scholars upon the way of the Salaf to take knowledge from and adhere to, because freedom from deviations in beliefs of their general methodology is only found to a comprehensive degree with the scholars upon this methodology. Additionally the actual situation bears witness that this is true.

23. From among these principles and characteristics of those upon the way of the pious predecessors and those Muslims who followed them in goodness, is that they do not consider any of the leaders of the people of innovation and falsehoods as revivers of the religion, even if they have acquired an amount of Sharee'ah knowledge. This is because from the affirmed characteristics of the revivers of Islaam, which is indispensable and without question is that he has both correct beliefs and the sound methodology upon knowledge.

And Allaah the Most High, knows best, may the praise and salutations of Allaah be upon our Prophet Muhammad, and upon his family, and his Companions.

(7)

EIGHTY-NINE BRIEF BENEFITS
RELATED TO THE METHODOLOGY
OF ISLAAM

01. The axis upon which this religion turns, and the foundation upon which it rests, is adherence to revealed guidance.

02. Allaah, the Most Glorified and the Most Exalted, has commanded the people to enter into Islaam completely and fully. As He, Allaah, the Most Perfect, has said, ❧ *Oh you who believe! Enter perfectly in Islaam (by obeying all the rules and regulations of the Islaamic religion)...* ❧-(Surah al-Baqarah: 208) If a worshiper of Allaah does not obey the Messenger, may Allaah's praise and salutations be upon him, nor hold firmly to the guidance of his Sunnah, then that worshiper has not entered into Islaam completely and fully.

03. From the most essential distinctive characteristics of the methodology of the first three righteous generations of Muslims is continually returning and referring back to the authentic evidences in the Sharee'ah and the established principles and fundamentals within it.

04. The greatest blessing we can have is that of beneficial knowledge and calling towards the truth. Allaah the Most High said, when informing us about 'Isaa, may Allaah's salutations be upon him, ❧ *And He has made me blessed wheresoever I be...* ❧-(Surah Maryam: 31) Blessed, meaning he was someone who conveyed and taught revealed knowledge to the people, bringing good to them wherever he was.

---

[1] These have been selected from the social media accounts of the Sheikh, may Allaah preserve him

05. The reason for some of the seekers of knowledge not successfully gaining knowledge is that they have failed to proceed in the same path in acquiring knowledge, and have not sought knowledge upon the same methodology which produced the people of knowledge among those who came before us.

06. Knowledge is not gained or acquired all at once, rather true knowledge is gained in levels, stage by stage.

07. Gaining knowledge requires determination and resolve, and that you do not allow yourself to become discouraged in your efforts and then simply say [I have studied and studied, but not really benefited!]

08. It is necessary for the student of knowledge to accustom himself to the fact that to truly gain knowledge it is necessary to spend whatever time is required to acquire it, and that he does not become discouraged when the length of time necessary becomes long.

09. If you seek knowledge upon the correct way and methodology it makes that objective which is far away something close, and that goal which is difficult something easier, and that distant aim something in fact nearby you. It brings into reality for the student true results and triumphs in his efforts, when he diligently follows the correct required steps.

10. 'Abdullah Ibn al-Mubaarak, may Allaah have mercy upon him, said, "**The first part of knowledge is sound intention, then properly listening to it, then understanding it, then acting according to it, then memorizing it carefully, then spreading and conveying it to others.**"

11. Oh student of knowledge, to be successful it is required that you proceed in acquiring knowledge just as the people of knowledge before you proceeded, step by step, stage by stage until after doing so you gain knowledge.

12. The Muslim Ummah needs two things: 1) Knowledge which is taken and received from those people who carry it meaning the verifying and clarifying scholars. 2) The distancing of ourselves from the people of misconceptions and false doubts in the religion.

13. Indeed, it is through knowledge that a Muslim is elevated and raised high, and it is by the lack of knowledge that he is lowered down and loses status and honor. As Allaah has said, ﴾ *Allaah will exalt in degree those of you who believe, and those who have been granted knowledge.* ﴿-(Surah al-Mujaadilah: 11)

14. The knowledge which was held and transmitted from the Companions of the Messenger, may Allaah be pleased with them, is in its entirety all beneficial knowledge. Whereas the knowledge coming from others contains that which is beneficial and well as that which may cause harm.

15. It is necessary that, during the early period of their youth, seekers of knowledge, spend their days, and their nights, fully engaging their intellects in studying and being focused upon the various issues of beneficial knowledge.

METHODOLOGY

16. Seeking knowledge is correctly considered a form of general worship. As such, it has been established that for any efforts of worship to be accepted by Allaah and for Allaah to grant a worshiper success through it what they do, that the one undertaking that specific effort or action be someone having complete sincerity of intention in undertaking that deed solely for the sake of Allaah the Most Exalted, the Most Magnificent.

17. As for the student of knowledge, if Allaah desires good for him, He guides the student to direct his attention towards clear unambiguous matters, to leave alone those difficult problems or issues which are complex, and to not pursue matters which are doubtful, as pursuing such matters leads to deviating towards misguidance, and we seek refuge in Allaah from that.

18. It is necessary that we affirm and adopt the clear unambiguous principles found within the Book of Allaah. Additionally, we must be aware of the greater objectives which some involved in the modern forms of media want for us, the Muslim Ummah, meaning that they aim to divide us and separate our unity as Muslims.

19. The Qur'aan is itself a methodology of guidance, and it supports our life upon guidance. It guides to the correct methodology in governing people's affairs and ruling between them in justice.

20. This Qur'aan is what elevated this Muslim Ummah, as Allaah says ❧ *And verily, this Qur'aan is indeed a Reminder for you (O Muhammad) and your people (Quraish people, or your followers), and you will be questioned about it.*❧ -(Surah az-Zukhruf: 44).

It was not raised to its position and status except through it. So it is upon you to praise your Lord for having sent down upon us this Qur'aan.

21. Allaah has made the guidance of the Qur'aan that which is intended to be directed towards addressing the sound intellect and legitimate human feeling and sentiments.

22. Oh memorizers of the Noble Qur'aan, indeed the Qur'aan has a right upon you that you act and reflect its guidance.

23. The command to obey the Messenger of Allaah, may Allaah's praise and salutations be upon him, is found within the Qur'aan in more than thirty different places. Each one of them contains the command to obey the Prophet, may Allaah's praise and salutations be upon him, and the prohibition against disobeying and opposing him.

24. The Sunnah, is a term which is a collective Arabic noun describing and encompassing everything which the Prophet, may Allaah's praise and salutations be upon him, was upon of both general and specific, from beliefs, acts of worship, and behaviors and ways of interacting.

25. Having faith or emaan that Muhammad is the Messenger of Allaah, may Allaah's praise and salutations be upon him, also increases and decreases. It increases through a Muslim's frequent efforts to adhere to the Prophet's Sunnah and it decreases through Muslims frequent acting in opposition to the Sunnah. As such the people having faith or emaan in the Prophet are not considered all being at the same level.

26. From the completeness in one's faith in the Prophet, may Allaah's praise and salutations be upon him, is that someone does not give general precedence to his own intellectual conclusions over the guidance of the Prophet's Sunnah, nor that you hold your own opinion which differs with anything which is Sunnah has specific guidance and judgment regarding.

27. Calling and inviting to beneficial knowledge, the Sunnah, and understanding that guidance which Allaah revealed to His Messenger, may Allaah's praise and salutations be upon him, is itself inviting and calling to unity upon the truth, and to the avoid separation and division.

28. The greatest of rewards someone might obtain are the rewards gained through tawheed, meaning properly establishing the worship of Allaah alone. The worst of evil someone may bring forth or produce is associating others with Allaah in that worship which is due to Him alone.

29. The attachment to knowledge, and the guidance of the Book and the Sunnah, as well as teaching the beneficial knowledge, is what directs the people towards adherence to the Sunnah, avoiding division, and holding firmly to the united body of Muslims upon the truth.

30. It is necessary for every Muslim to have the fundamental understanding that the adherence to the Sunnah is directly connected to and always related to holding firmly to the united body of Muslims upon the truth. Similarly, is the necessity of understanding that innovation in the religion is always related and connected to division and

separation from the truth. As it is said, "**Holding to the united body of Muslim upon the truth is a mercy, and separating from it is a punishment.**"

31. The command to adhere to the Sunnah is, from another direction, itself like a prohibition against innovating new matters into the religion. Similarly, the prohibition against innovations in the religion is from another direction itself like a command to adhere and hold firmly to the Sunnah in all matters of knowledge and belief.

32. Innovation in Islaam is whatever is introduced into the religion which opposes the evidenced path of the Prophet, may the praise and salutations of Allaah be upon him and his family, whether in knowledge, or in deeds and actions.

33. The Sunnah generally includes the correct beliefs, and also includes the requirement of following of the Prophet, may the praise and salutations of Allaah be upon him and his family, in everything considered worship, as well as all general commands and prohibitions.

34. From the most significant fundamentals of the religion of Islaam, and from the most important matters that we have been commanded with and encouraged with- is the urging of the worshiper of Allaah and his being commanded to adhere firmly to the Sunnah and to abandon innovation and division within the religion of Islaam.

35. The sound use of the intellect, making proper Sharee'ah analogies, and reaching correctly derived Sharee'ah opinions are all matters which serve and assist the authority of the Sunnah, yet they should never be consider equal or predominant over it to

any degree.

36. From the foundation of having emaan or faith in the Prophet, may the praise and salutations of Allaah be upon him, is to hold closely to his guidance, and hold firmly to his Sunnah. This holding firmly to his Sunnah encompasses matters that are related to knowledge and beliefs, as well as encompassing those which are related to actions and deeds.

37. The various witnesses aspects of the revival of the Muslim Ummah and its current revival it is an important and essential aspect of the needed development and formation of a comprehensive understanding of knowledge which reflects Islaam.

38. From the valid descriptions in narrations of those Muslims who will be considered strangers at different periods and times in history is that that ones who disobey and oppose them in what they call to are much more numerous than those who obey what they call to within society. From this characteristic, it can be understood that they are not only those who have restricted the guidance of Islaam to themselves by adhering firmly to Islaam and the Sunnah, but that they also are involved in calling others to its guidance.

39. Calling to Allaah and His religion can be through efforts of writing and authoring, and it can be calling through speaking and engaging in discussions, and it can also be through the giving of sound advice and similar efforts.

40. It is obligatory upon every Muslim to be content and accepting of the guidance from the Messenger, upon him be Allaah's praise and salutations, in every aspect of what he has been given, as the guidance he has been given is only revelation from Allaah revealed to him. Even if there is some affirmed matter which is disconcerting to your mind, know that it is still a matter based upon relation revealed to him, may Allaah's praise and salutations be upon him.

41. Those who adhere to the Sunnah, hold firmly to it with their molar teeth, and are patient with whatever is connected to doing so- are those who are truly free. Additionally they are those who are described with praise as the strangers upon the Sunnah, even if the people clearly oppose the Sunnah.

42. The periodic strangeness of Islaam is relative and variable through history. It may be found to be seen as strange in one age but not in another age, or it may be found to be strange in one location of the world but not in another.

43. It is understood from the authentic narrations describing the "Strangers" that Islaam will become something honored and influential after being strange, since in the initial state it was first strange but then after that initial strangeness Islaam and its people became honored and strong.

44. The hadeeth states, {...*and it will return to being something strange as it began.*} meaning that true authentic Islaam will again return to being something strange. Its fundamentals and principles will return to a state of being considered strange among people, at different times and points in

history.

45. From the outward strangeness of those who adhere to the Sunnah, is the strangeness of those upright people involved in acquiring knowledge. These are those who seek Sharee'ah knowledge for Allaah's sake alone, as distinguished from those who seek Sharee'ah knowledge for other than the sake of Allaah, meaning that they only do so for the sake of their standing in society, or wealth, or gaining a position above others.

46. If the correct way and direction to follow in some matter is not clear to you and you are uncertain of what to do, then search and investigate what was the way taken by the Prophet, may the praise and salutations of Allaah be upon him, and his Companions.

47. The person who turns away from the Sunnah and wants to follow other ways which conflict or oppose the Sunnah, is indeed someone who has chosen to refuse to enter Jannah in the Hereafter.

48. Sinning and transgressing can be through the commission of what is known to be a major sin, but it also can be what occurs that is less than this, meaning occurring when someone frequently rejects the Sunnah and refuses to give attention to its guidance.

49. That advice which I offer to myself first and foremost, as well as to every Muslim, is that he accustom himself to accepting whatever comes from the authentic Sunnah, and to believe whatever is authentic from the Sunnah as transmitted from the Prophet, may the praise and salutations of Allaah be upon him and his family.

50. The correct definition of extremism is: that which goes beyond the limits of what a Muslim has been commanded to do in the Sharee'ah. The one who goes beyond the proper limits in some matter, whether criticizing some wrongdoing from others or in performing acts of worship oneself, outside of or beyond what the Sharee'ah itself allows, he is from the people involved in extremism.

51. The Prophet, upon him be Allaah's praise and salutations, blamed and criticized those three individuals in his time who leaned towards extremism in their performance of acts of worship. Therefore, if any matter does not conform to the Sunnah and its guidance, it is something which is rejected from whoever does it, even if their intention and goal was sincere and good.

52. If a young Muslim is initially cultivated upon a sound understanding of the Book of Allaah and the Sunnah, then there will be no weaknesses or faulty gaps in his understanding and practice of the Sharee'ah which could be affected by extremism, negligence, or any involvement with forms of terrorism.

53. It is an obligation upon the people of knowledge to not neglect clarifying matters, in light in the presence today of deviated concepts and beliefs, as well as the presence of modern groups which stand upon the same methodology of previously acknowledged misguided sects, who legitimized attacking and killing those people which the Sharee'ah does not justify fighting militarily.

54. The pure true Sharee'ah, meaning based upon the Book of Allaah and the Sunnah, prohibits extremism even to the extent of when a person deals with his own self. Being extreme with one's own self is prohibited in the hadeeth narration of the three men who went beyond the guidance of the Sunnah in worship in which the Messenger says, *{Whoever turns away from my Sunnah is not of me... }*

55. The pure and true Sharee'ah as transmitted in the Book of Allaah, the authentic Sunnah, and the life history of the Prophet, may the praise and salutations of Allaah be upon him, naturally nullifies extremism through the combination of many different aspects of what the Sharee'ah itself calls for. This is in relation to correct belief, in acts of worship, in personal behavior, as well as in what it advocates for the well-being of society generally which are clearly distinct from terrorism.

56. The guiding ruling within the hadeeth *{Whoever turns away from my Sunnah is not of me.}* clearly applies to the various newly developed innovated methodologies of calling and establishing the religion which do not have a clear basis within the Sunnah, and which have come forth in our modern age.

57. It is an obligation upon a Muslim to accept and affirm every statement of the Prophet, may Allaah's praise and salutations be upon him. He must free himself from anything which his desires invites to of giving precedence to his own intellectual conclusions and his personal views above what has been authentically stated by the Prophet, may Allaah's praise and salutations be upon him.

58. Whoever within his own affairs, adheres to the guidance of the Prophet, may the praise and salutations of Allah be upon him, calls and invites to it through his actions and endeavors.

59. The hadeeth narration, *{One who guides to something good has a reward similar to that of its doer.}* is something which indicates the validity of the principle: '**The means connected to achieving matters have the same ruling as those intended matters themselves.**'

60. Regarding the correct way that we must assess different individuals, and how we weigh and assess various matters as Muslims, we should not be deceived by only looking at outward appearances. Rather we must look closely into the inward root of the affair and fundamental foundation which it stands upon. This is done by asking, "Is this matter or what they are doing something which adheres to and follows the Sunnah or not?" and "Is there an established Sunnah which supports this or not?"

61. If an individual wants to ensure that his supplications do not include anything that goes beyond the boundaries of what is correct, then he shouldn't simply devise new supplications from his own thoughts, but should give preference to using those supplications coming from the Messenger of Allaah, as well is those which have been transmitted by the Companions of the prophet, and the guided scholars.

62. It is an obligation upon the students of knowledge and the callers to the religion to be models and examples to the people, specifically when different current events are happening within society and

general people's understanding and perceptions of these affairs become confused and unclear.

63. It is required that the worshipper direct and turn himself toward the One who has perfect attributes, and lofty and most beautiful characteristics, that being only Allaah the Most Perfect and the Most High.

64. Allaah the Most High said, ❖ *...This day, I have perfected your religion for you, completed My Favor upon you, and have chosen for you Islaam as your religion....*❖-(Surah al-Ma'idah: 3). As such, in light of this verse, the one who brings forth something new and without basis in the religion itself, is claiming that the religion has not been completed for us.

65. The one who undertakes the means used to achieve a praiseworthy objective, and the means he used is acceptable in the Sharee'ah, then he will be rewarded for that effort put forth using that accepted means, separate from that reward connected to actually obtaining the praiseworthy objective. Just as Allaah the Most High says, ❖ *Nor do they spend anything (in Allaah's Cause) - small or great - nor cross a valley, but is written to their credit...* ❖-(Surah al-Tawbah:121)

66. What is written in the mentioned records of life possessed by the angels for individuals, whether that is pertaining to a single day or for the year, contains general information within which it is possible that some future variations occur in what has been written generally. But, as for the records which are stated in the Lawh al-Mafudh it is not liable to any variation at all and contains every possible matter in

detail. This is one of the meanings of the statement, **'Allaah wipes out whatever He wished, and He also makes some matters unchangeable.'**

67. The categories of people who enter into Jannah are two: those who enter Jannah straightaway after Judgment and those who enter into it at a later time from those people that will be placed into Hellfire first. This second category will suffer some of the punishment of Hellfire to the degree of their own previous evil deeds and wrongdoings, before eventually entering Jannah afterwards due to their worship.

68. Allaah, the Most Glorified and the Most Exalted, alone is the one who brings forth all matters of good, and He alone is the One who directs away from any worshiper matters of evil and harm. He is the One who brings about all good and blessings upon His worshipers, and He is the One who turns away from His worshipers any harm that might reach them.

69. Allaah the Most High said, ◈ *Verily! Man (disbeliever) is ungrateful to his Lord . And to that he bears witness (by his deeds).* ◈-(Surah al-'Aadiyaat:6-7) meaning he shows this through his what his actions say and reflect, meaning his outward deeds, that he is ungrateful and unappreciative to the many blessing given to him by Allaah, the Most High.

70. The believer is one whose heart holds and keeps encouragements towards righteousness that holds humbleness and fear of Allaah the Most High. From that which it is suitable for the worshiper of Allaah is that he distance himself from the causes of arrogance, the causes of one's heart becoming

hard, and from being seduced and occupied by the inviting aspects of worldly pleasures.

71. The sound intellect confirms what is authentically transmitted from revealed knowledge. Through it, the sound intellect is able to reach the goal of properly understanding matters and general affairs.

72. The hadeeth narration, {*Allaah is Gentle and loves gentleness in all things.*}meaning in how things are done, and how they are carried out, in the general managing and governing of our affairs, and in dealing with those we agree with as well as in dealing those who we have a specific disagreement with.

73. Allaah the Most High said, ◈ *When the Event (i.e. the Day of Resurrection) befalls.* ◈-(Surah al-Waaqi'ah: 1) Al-Waaqi'ah is from of the affirmed names for the Day of Judgment. There are a number of names for the Day of Judgment due to it having several different fundamental characteristics. Moreover, the fact that something has many names is an indication of its significance and importance.

74. Allaah the Most High said, ◈ *And obey Allaah and the Messenger (Muhammad) that you may obtain mercy.* ◈-(Surah Aal-Imraan: 132) Certainly, the reason and direct cause for the pouring of Allaah's mercy over His worshipers is their obedience to Allaah and His Messenger, may Allaah's praise and salutations be upon him.

75. In relation to physical objects the blessing Allaah has placed within them are of two different types, those which posses as essential blessing by themselves due to who they came from, and those that have blessing when they are used properly. In our Sharee'ah the only physical things that are considered essentially

blessed by themselves are only those physically connected to the persons of the prophets and messengers in their specific time and age. For this reason, it was permissible for Muslims to seek the blessings from what was actually affirmed to be the hair of the Prophet Muhammad, or when he was alive from his perspiration, and whatever is similar from those physical things which connected directly to him.

76. It was from the guidance of the first three generation of believers that whenever they come toward something from the fruits of this world they would fear for themselves regarding any negative effect upon them, moreover they would not be prideful or brag about it. Rather they would sincerely seek success in being able to use it to gain the pleasure of Allaah.

77. Having pride is generally something blameworthy, except in regarding to the blessing of emaan, the having of taqwa and properly fearing Allaah, and the blessing of righteousness.

78. Patience is to control and hold the tongue back from complaining about what misfortunes have occurred, and to inwardly control one's heart suppressing discontent with what happened, and to outwardly refrain and stop your limbs and body from showing any discontent, whether that might have been shown through the practice of some peoples of striking their face and cheeks, tearing their clothes, or whatever forbidden acts similar to these.

79. Precision in carefully taking and adopting points of knowledge results in producing a sound intellect which properly understands and considers matters.

80. Confusion and chaos in one's mind and intellect produces the results of a life only concerned with material things, a life merely focused upon desires and the seeking of enjoyment.

81. Wealth in the religion of Islaam has a significant position and role when it is used as a means necessary to bring about good. For this reason, the pillar of zakaat is mentioned alongside the essential pillar of the ritual prayer in many different places where salaat is mentioned in the Book and the Sunnah.

82. Surah Yusuf has been named by some of the scholars, like Ibn Taymeeyah, as Surah ad-Da'wah. This is because it contains within it discussions about the life path of a caller to Allaah, about the call to worship Allaah alone, about the essential fundamentals of calling others towards Allaah, about the conditions and circumstances usually encountered in calling to the truth, and descriptions of the changing situations and circumstances that a caller to Allaah may pass through in his efforts.

83. In relation to the realm of calling and inviting to Allaah and His path, the characteristic of following of guidance closely and turning away from developing new matters, are from the most essential distinctive characteristics of the methodology and path adhered to by the first three righteous generations of Muslims.

84. The correct belief in any matter is established by even a single sound authentic evidence. However bringing forth multiple sound evidences more effectively cuts off and refutes the sources and basis of the unreasonable claims and far-fetched assertions put forth by those who are misguided. It also negates and nullifies the false conclusions reached through the misinterpretations which the false and misguided sects adopt and chose to proceed upon.

85. From the most serious of transgressions and crimes in Islaam is causing division among the Muslims. Likewise, from the most important foundations which the Prophet, may Allaah's praise and salutations be upon him, called to was having unity in Islaam upon the truth, and being united practically in acting and staying together, and the avoidance of differing and separating.

86. A person is not safe and secure in his religion if he is someone who becomes pleased with something which is known to be wrong doing or sin, or if he finds that there appears within himself those ideas or notions that make light or diminish the importance of some affirmed matter which is clearly acknowledged as wrongdoing in Islaam.

87. Allaah the Most High said, ❧ *And do not do mischief on the earth, after it has been set in order* ❧-(Surah al-A'raf: 56). A group of scholars from the early righteous generations explain this to mean, "Do not spread corruption on the earth by engaging in the association of others with Allaah in worship, or by openly engaging in acts of wrongdoing and sin, after its lands had become rectified through being established upon the worship of Allaah alone and the promotion of acts of goodness and righteousness."

88. The righteous first generations of Islaam agreed that the doubts and misconceptions in the religion found among the people, and their harmful effect upon their practice of the religion were more significant and severe than the effects among them caused by wrongfully following their worldly desires. As misconceptions and doubts which are connected to understanding the religion become established and remain firmly in what they hold, whereas worldly desires come and go readily according to whether the one who fell into them has repented from them or not.

89. It is an obligation that we make the masjids places used for the spreading of beneficial knowledge taken from the Book of Allaah and the Sunnah and from the transmitted statements of the righteous first three generations of Islaam. They should not be places where the speech of: the people of innovation in the religion, the people who stand in opposition to the guidance of Islaam, or the people who have separated from the guided Muslims and are following their desires, are allowed to be spread.

(8)

STEPS TO CORRECTLY ADDRESS SOMEONE'S ERROR IN THE RELIGION

heikh Muhammad Ibn 'Umar Baazmool, may Allaah preserve him, explains the guidance of the Sunnah in how we differ with people and we differ about, and what our perspective should be in these different situation. The first important distinction is to distinguish between matters which Islaam has guidance for and those matters outside of the guidance of Islaam,[1]

"Know that you should allow someone else the acceptable range of free choice to form their own opinion and differ from you specifically in those matters which do not oppose the guidance of the Sharee'ah. If someone differed with a personal conclusion or opinion you have adopted know that you should allow someone else the acceptable range of free choice to form their own opinion and differ from you- specifically in those matters which do not oppose the guidance of the Sharee'ah, and teach yourself to accept this.

Work with the one who differs from your taken opinion by respecting his opinion, since the nature of the issue which is not connected to the Sharee'ah is that it is not something determined and clear-cut. This is for example in the affairs of world matters which have no connection at all to the revealed Sharee'ah guidance. Such that the one who differs with your opinion in this area is not someone you should get angry with, but interact with him recognizing that they have a similar free choice to form an opinion in non-religious matters, and accept that from them.

This also includes those issues actually connected to the Sharee'ah in those matters in which there is not definitive evidence, or in which there are evidences that outwardly appear to conflict or differ. In this situation also, the individual who chooses an evidenced position

---

[1] From the Facebook page of Sheikh Muhammad Ibn 'Umar Baazmool

different with the position you have chosen as correct; you should not be harsh or censure him due to it, but rather accept that position from him, acknowledging that he has the freedom to choose what he holds is supported as the most correct. And the success in this and all is with Allaah."

The sheikh, may Allaah reward him, has also discussed in further detail and offered an outline of dealing and handling the situation where we differ with another Muslim in those matters directly connected to our blessed religion, saying,[2]

---

[2]   From the Facebook page of Sheikh Muhammad Ibn 'Umar Baazmool

"The first step is understanding and recognizing the reality that every son and daughter of Aadam makes mistakes and errors, and the best of those who make mistakes are the ones who repent.[3] This is the first step towards properly dealing with others mistakes, whether it is a Muslim who follows the first generations that falls into it or someone else.

THE SECOND STEP

Look and precisely consider the mistake which that person fell into.[4] Is their mistake within the realm of those issues where the scholars have needed to independently consider the relevant evidences and derive their rulings from them? Or is the issue a matter in which the Sharee'ah evidences are clear and definitive and such that it is required that everyone accept it?

For the general Muslim, clarifying this requires referring to a student of knowledge or a scholar whom we can return that matter which our brother differs with us about in order to ask. We might say, "*So and so has made such and such mistake sheikh. How do we work with him? What should our position towards him be because of this?*"

As it may in fact be the case that the matter which the brother holds, which we differ with him about, could be from the matters that required scholars to independently consider the evidences and so they have reached different

---

[3] This is the direct meaning of an authentic hadeeth of the Prophet, may the praise and salutations of Allaah be upon him

[4] Part of what should be done here was mentioned by Sheikh al-'Utheimeen, may Allaah the Most High, have mercy upon him, in a gathering between Sheikh Rabee'a Ibn Haadee and Sheikh al-'Utheimeen, "*It is required that you confirm the matter first, then engage in a discussion with the one who made this false statement or misguided position. If after this he still rejects what is correct and persists upon falsehood, then he is openly refuted and his error explained publicly so that the people are not deceived into accepting his mistake. It is obligatory to first confirm accurately what was said, then secondly discuss the matter between the one wishing to clarify and the one from whom this misguidance was reported. After confirmation, if he rejects and persists what he stands upon of falsehood, then clarify openly what the truth is.*" .

conclusions regarding it. In this case, it is not that he is differing with us in an issue which there is no other proper option but to follow the single position which the Sharee'ah evidence clearly points towards.

For this reason, the manner in which we deal and interact with him, due to it being a type of issue in which there are legitimate differences since it required independent scholastic assessments from the scholars, is not the same matter as if his opposition to the correct position was in a religious matter in which the definite evidence required a single position be adopted. He, for example, could differ with us in the issue of where to place the hands after bowing in a rakaat of ritual prayer. Meaning that he places them back onto his chest and we do not do so, or the opposite, we place them back there after bowing and he does not do so. As this is a matter that has been explained differently by reliable scholars whose conclusions were upon evidence.

Or it could be for example, in the matter of the best length for a man's 'izar or lower garment to reach, such that he holds the position that the best place is the middle of the calf and so always wears his thobe to that point. Yet we might hold that the acceptable length for a man's 'izar or lower garment, is what the Messenger of Allaah, may the praise and salutations of Allaah be upon him, mentioned " A believer's garment is best at the middle of the calf, there is no blame upon him for what lies between there and above his two ankles, and whatever is below the ankles is in the Hellfire." He may differ with us in this issue, as he only wear his garments to the middle of the shin whereas we accept wearing it in a way that may also reach to the top of the ankles.

Or the difference could be in an issue such as the ruling on wearing an imaamah or turban. We do not hold that it is legislated to wear a turban specifically as a garment, but we do wear head garments, one of which is generally linguistically called a khimaar, which, when worn by Muslim men, we specially call a "ghutarah" or "shamaagh". This is one of those issues which are understood to have several legitimate understandings about it, since there is no definitive evidence indicating one position or which supports a specific position held by scholars or someone's view.

Or the difference could be the issue of them holding that the person who does not perform the ritual prayer is a disbeliever generally, without any specification or restrictions upon this ruling. Whereas we might hold that the person who leaves performing the ritual prayer out of laziness and general negligence does not immediately fall into disbelief, but if they turn away from the ritual prayer by knowingly denying its obligation in Islaam, then this person clearly becomes a disbeliever. This latter position would be due to taking a detailed ruling which is what the majority of the scholars have done in this issue. But regarding such types of differences it is not proper that there be any disputes, as these are matters of disagreement where both positions are legitimate and given consideration, and both positions have evidence to support them.

Consequently, this step requires more significant understanding and understanding of the boundaries of legitimate differences in Islaam. As has been said by some: When an individual's knowledge of what are legitimate differences increases his heart becomes more at ease, and when an individual has a deficiency in understanding the boundaries of legitimate differences his chest comes to be tighter and restricted.

In regard to the mistake that has occurred from a brother, if you recognize that he has made a mistake which is not from the area of evidence-based differences and that it is in fact required that he adopt the single correct position, then we do censure and blame him for this. We have some sternness with him and enjoin upon him the accepting of what is correct and forbid him from holding what is from error or wrongdoing. We also enjoin upon him returning and referring back to the scholars or to suitable students of knowledge in order that what is correct in this disputed issue, be explained to him.

Whereas if his position had been one in area of evidence-based differences, then we would convey what we hold to be the correct position, discuss it kindly, advise him, and talk with him gently in a good way, without acting harshly with him because of nature of this difference between us.

THE FOURTH STEP

It is required that we avoid and stay away from any going beyond the bounds of what is proper when arguing. As some of the people, are not able to stand that someone differs with them in any matter at all. This type of person falls into excessiveness and going beyond what is proper when arguing, such that whenever someone disagrees with him in an issue he goes to extremes in opposing him.

This is from the signs of characteristics of the hypocrites. Since the Messenger of Allaah, may the praise and salutations of Allaah be upon him, said, *{Four characteristics constitute anyone who possesses them a sheer hypocrite, and anyone who possesses one of them possesses a characteristics of hypocrisy till he abandons it : when he talks he lies, when he makes a promise he violates it, when he makes* *a covenant he acts treacherously, and when he quarrels, he deviates from what is true and the truth.}* Going beyond the bounds of the truth when arguing due to a difference is from the clear characteristics of the hypocrites, so it is upon a Muslim to be warned away from this.

THE FIFTH STEP

This is having dialogs and discussing issues with him, and also our bringing the matter of his opposition to what is correct from the Sharee'ah to the people of knowledge. We should ask him to refer to the people of knowledge for clarification in this. We should have students of knowledge speak with him, advising him, explaining the evidences to him, establishing the proof of the matter to him, and removing any doubts and misconceptions that he may have. Additionally it should also be made clear to him the danger of standing as someone who follows his desires in a matter of our religion!

After this point of the evidences having been presented and made clear to him, and he then rejects it,[5] it is important to state, that we are moving from the general level of putting forth a Sharee'ah description of stating that his statement is in error, or that his action is incorrect or that he has opposed what is sound, to a specific description that he is someone involved in innovation. This could also be to an even more serious position of stating that his condition is that of an innovator in the religion, and that he is misguided and that he is from those people who generally only follow their desires. We

[5]   In Tabaqaat al-Hanaabilah, Imaam Ahmad was asked about an individual from among the people with knowledge who falls into error, how does he repent to Allaah from it? Imaam Ahmad replied,*"Allaah will not accept his repentance from that until - he makes apparent and clear his repentance from it, retracting what he said, announcing that he previously made such and such incorrect statement and he now sincerely repents to Allaah the Most High from his statement of error and accepts what is shown to be correct. If these matters all come forth then his repentance is accepted."* Then he recited the verse, *"Except those who repent and do righteous deeds, and openly declare (the truth which they concealed). These, I will accept their repentance."*-(Surah al-Baqarah: 160)

171

are moving from a general description of the mistake and error which opposes the guidance of the Sharee'ah to a specific attribution of that to them as an individual, after establishing that a sufficient clarification of what is correct has been made.

Thereafter, it becomes necessary that we undertake another matter since we now recognize the danger of such an individual. Since he is now, after clarification, clearly standing as someone knowingly carrying false concepts that are not justified that he clings to. He is opposing the way of the people of the Sunnah and adherence to the Jamaa'ah. Therefore, it is then necessary and proper that we limit the harmful effect of that wrongdoing and evil he stands upon among others, and prevent that from affecting people generally. This is accomplished through publicly abandoning him, warning away from him, away from those who choose to continue to sit with him, listen to him, and read his books.

Since with such an individual, whom the proofs have been established against directly, remaining silent about him, only enables him to spread and propagate his incorrect concepts and false thinking to others. He may have a negative effect among beginning students of knowledge to the degree that it may eventually cause them to stray away from the Sunnah completely. For this reason our remaining silent would allow the spread of his misconceptions, only contributing to the people being directed towards misguidance and away from the clear way of the people of the Sunnah and adherence to the Jamaa'ah.

There is a tremendous principle which the first generations of Islaam affirmed, to the degree that it is narrated that they stood upon consensus in affirming it. That principle is the requirement of generally abandoning the people of innovation and those who have taken a path of following their desires in the religion.

As such, we abandon and warn against them. We do not sit with them nor with those associated with them, nor listen to them, or cooperate in any way that strengthens their ranks and efforts, rather we generally distance ourselves from them. Since, after the proofs and evidences have been clearly conveyed and explained, he stands as someone knowingly involved in innovation and misguidance. It should be noted that there is no distinction about innovations from him, meaning whether they are small or large innovations in the religion, since every innovation is from misguidance, and those individuals knowingly upon that are considered people of misguidance.

This is the way and methodology of the people of the Sunnah and adherence to the Jamaa'ah in working with those people who have fallen into an error in the religion. Additionally, there has in this age appeared a group of people who have adopted the perspective of the Khawaarij and the incorrect approach of the sect of the Khawaarij in dealing and interacting with someone who has fallen into an error or mistake as a Muslim. What exactly is it that this new group does? This new group directly rules upon the person who falls into error, as if he is someone knowingly upon that error, without establishing the proofs and evidences against him to support that.

Furthermore, they do not properly distinguish between someone generally following the Sunnah who makes an error and someone from one of the misguided sects who makes an error in the religion. Neither do they differentiate between the well-known scholar upon the Sunnah, who, despite his error, generally adheres to the Book of Allaah and the Sunnah, and between a person openly involved in innovation and forms of misguidance. They wrongly treat and handle them as equal or the same situation. These are those that are called "Hadaadees", and their approach opposes the approach of the people of the

Sunnah and adherence to the Jamaa'ah in this area of the religion. They have gone beyond what the people of the Sunnah and adherence to the Jamaa'ah stand upon in this subject and area, so it is proper to warn against them and not follow their incorrect approach.

This important task of clarification and indicating what is correct also applies to those who attach themselves to the Sunnah. Clarifying errors of those who attribute themselves to the way of the first Muslims is not attacking them as some wrongly believe, upon the condition that the guidelines of Islaam are followed when clarifying matters according to the specifics of the situation."

DEALING WITH ERRORS FROM SOMEONE FOLLOWING THE FIRST GENERATIONS

Clarifying the importance of some detailed aspects of dealing with differences among that occur between the people who adhere to the Sunnah, Sheikh 'Ubayd Ibn 'Abdullah al-Jaabiree, may Allaah preserve him, mentioned that,[6]

> *"It is obligatory of the Sunnee to generally preserve the honor of another Sunnee, and it is obligatory upon the Salafee to safeguard another Salafee, and protect his honor. Just as it is upon him to not pursue his brothers' mistakes if he slips and makes a mistake. As the people of the Sunnah look at the nature and degree of the error which has been fallen into just as they look and consider the state of the one who made the error.*

> *Firstly, it is clearly affirmed that a mistake or error is clarified and refuted, not accepted. As it is possible for one who is Salafee to make a mistake, and differ with another Salafee in some matters in which he is, in fact, incorrect. As the one who adheres to the way of*

ERRORS

[6]   As taken from several related post transcription on Sahab.net

the Salaf is also human, and makes mistakes as humans do. After affirming this, the people of the Sunnah look and consider the individual who fell into a mistake. If the person who made a mistake is someone upon the Sunnah, connected to it, and known for preceding upon the Sunnah; then the one differing with him should not search out his errors, and generally preserves his honor when clarifying.

If the person is someone from the people upon innovation into the religion, then they are not due the concern for preserving their honor. As such, based upon this, we say that it is upon the Salafees, upon the people of the Sunnah, when there are differences, to open their hearts towards one another, and that they enter into discussions between themselves about the differences that have occurred between them, and that they lay out and present the different issues in which they differ among themselves to those who are more capable and qualified than them from among the people of knowledge, from those scholars who are those standing upon the Sunnah. Through undertaking this, the differences will be able to be removed, their word unified, and their ranks joined together if Allaah, the Most High, so wills, and they will be able to hold together in unity."

Sheikh 'Ubayd al-Jaabiree, may Allaah preserve him, discussed dealing with those who are mistaken in some matters but adhere to the methodology of the first Muslims,[7]

"...It is obligatory upon the Salafees to deal with each other gently, and act with deliberation, and not hastily resort to the Sharee'ah practice of abandonment with each other, as this is a mistake. Without question, the one who opposes what is correct and sound is refuted,

---

[7]   From the audio cassette 'Question of the Young Muslim men from the City of Birmingham in Britain'

he is refuted and his error is not accepted. If an individual has made a mistake related to the religion, then clarify that error, by showing with evidence what is correct and that the truth opposes his position or statement.

As for the practice of abandonment, it should be utilized for abandoning the innovator who has had the proof clearly establish against him, and still makes his innovation apparent and open. Such an individual is abandoned and not treated with any honor, except when practicing abandonment with him specifically results in a greater corruption and harm than not implementing it. Then, in this case, it is sufficient to simply warn against him, and warn against sitting with him, without abandoning him completely, where you would even refuse to give him the greeting of salaam, and other similar actions.

The reality is that many of the Salafees act with severity with their brothers in this matter, of abandonment, according to what we have been informed of. The position they adopt is often simply due to what one Salafee sees from his brothers of making a statement that he is not pleased with, and so he chooses to abandon him. And this in reality is not suitable nor proper, and is a mistake."

He also, may Allaah preserve him, explained that, [8]

"We do not accept errors or mistakes in relation to the affairs of the religion, nor can we simply overlook or justify them from someone because the individual is Salafee. Any mistake related to the religion is clarified with a knowledge-based clarification. If it is possible to first advise this brother of ours who is Salafee that his position and statement, in this issue of so-and-so is

---

[8]   As quoted from the book 'A Friendly Caution from the Mistakes Made by Sheikh Saaleh Sadlaan'

mistaken, then this is excellent. If that is not practically possible then we openly clarify that he has opposed what is correct in this position or issue.

However, we do not deal with an error coming from a Salafee the same way we deal with an error coming from one of the people of innovation in the religion, since being upon innovation- he is generally spoken against. The Salafee upon error should not be defamed, not warned from absolutely, not treated harshly with a harshness that dismisses all of his efforts and his position influence upon the efforts of calling to the way of the first three generations. Doing that, is in reality, excessiveness, and an oppression, meaning an injustice, which is unacceptable."

And the success is with Allaah.

(9)

LEARN BENEFICIAL KNOWLEDGE FROM ITS PEOPLE & CONVEY IT

GUIDANCE RELATED TO GAINING & ACQUIRING KNOWLEDGE

One of the challenges many Muslims face due to not having the opportunity to take knowledge and understanding of Islaam directly from the steadfast scholars directly is confusion regarding important aspects of both acquiring knowledge and conveying it others. Sheikh Muhammad Baazmool, may Allaah preserve him, was asked, ***Question: What is the correct understanding of and comprehension of those distinguishing matters which are found in the statement of Allaah, ◈ So ask of those who know the Scripture, if you know not.◈- (Surah an-Nahl: 43)*** In his response he clarifies several important fundamentals and distinctions about this,[1]

*"All praise is due to Allaah. May Allaah's praise and salutations be upon the noblest of prophets and messengers, our leader Muhammad, and upon his household, and Companions. As for what follows: Indeed Allaah the Most High says, ◈ **So ask of those who know the Scripture, if you know not.** ◈-(Surah an-Nahl: 43). This indicates a number of different matters.*

The first matter: All the Muslims are considered to be of one of two categories, the category of those who are the people of knowledge, and those who are not from among the people of knowledge; these are generally called common Muslims.

The second matter: From what this verse indicates is that it is the job and function of the people of knowledge to clarify and explain matters. Correspondingly, it is the job of the general Muslims to return and ask the people of knowledge about whatever matters they do not

[1]   'Questions on the Methodology of Islaam by phone' from bazmool.net

understand or need an explanation of.

The third matter: From what this verse indicates is that the people of knowledge are considered those of knowledge due to what they posses of the "dhikr" or scripture. What is meant by "dhikr" or scripture is the Qur'aan and Sunnah as properly understood by the righteous preceding first generations of this Ummah. That scholar who is truly described as having knowledge of the Qur'aan and authentic hadeeth narrations and following what the transmitted reports of the righteous predecessors convey, he is considered from among the ranks of the people of knowledge who were indicated by Allaah, the Most Perfect and the Most High in this specific verse.

The fourth matter, this verse indicates the position that it is not from the place of the general people to challenge the scholars in these matters of the religion. Rather in fact it is upon the general Muslim to follow the guidance of the scholars. Such that if a scholar indicates a commanded matter then it is required upon the general Muslims to follow them and take hold of their statements of guidance. It is not permissible for a common Muslim if he specifically goes to a scholar for ruling, that he then opposes that ruling which he hears from the scholar, except when that ruling opposes a clear verse of the Qur'aan, in authentic narration, or position established upon verified Consensus within the Muslim Ummah.

The fifth matter, indicated by this verse, ❖ **So ask of those who know the Scripture, if you know not.** ❖ *-(Surah an-Nahl: 43) is if those people do not refer and turn to the people of knowledge but instead adhere to their personal conceived positions and simply follow their own desires, or follow and obey those individuals* *who are not considered from among the people of knowledge, then they are proceeding in a way which opposes the commands of Allaah the Most High. As Allah has said,* ❖*...And let those who oppose the Messenger's (Muhammad) commandment (i.e. his Sunnah legal ways, orders, acts of worship, statements, etc.) (among the sects) beware, lest some trials or afflictions befall them or a painful torment be inflicted on them* ❖*-(Surah an-Nur: 63). And Allaah knows best"*

He was similarly asked a question that adds detail to how we ask for guidance,[2] *"A question our sheikh, may Allaah increase you in goodness, some of the general people chose or select who they wish to go to ask rulings from. Such that they take the ruling about this issue from one scholar and another issue is taken from a different scholar, so what is your guidance about this practice? Is it acceptable for a general Muslims to chose whomever he wishes to ask for a ruling from the scholars? Then can he take their ruling in any situation or case.*

Or is what is correct the practice that you mentioned previously, that ('What is required from the general Muslims is that he ask about those matters he does not have knowledge of, asking the people of knowledge f the Book of Allah and the Sunnah whom he knows are reliable in their knowledge, piety, and fear of Allaah. If they inform him of the rulings of the religion then he should accept their statements...')"

"It is not in fact required that a Muslim only stick to the statements of only one certain scholar specifically, with him not being able to ask anyone else nor refer to any other scholar. Rather he should ask whomever it is easy for him to ask from those who are accurately described as those with knowledge or the people of knowledge. If a suitable scholar informs him about the

issue, but if is one that the scholars have differed about, and is one that required the scholars themselves to make an independent scholastic determination, and one which among the different scholastic positions there is not a definitive source text that would obligate him to chose one of the different positions, then he can chose from those positions upon the condition that those from whom he is taking their statements are truly from the people of knowledge of the Book of Allah and the Sunnah, and that the scholar is from the people suitable for issuing rulings in such matters, being someone of both piety and knowledge. And Allaah knows best"

It is important to also understand what we should do in the common situation of many who are Muslim minorities in western countries in a land or region with no scholars. He, was also asked,[3] "**May Allaah bless you, our sheikh. On some countries there is not even those students of knowledge whom the scholars have recommended, not to speak of there possibly being scholars there to take from. As such what is the suitable course of action in such situations our sheikh?**

*"The proper course of action in this case is that the people refer back to the scholars whom are outside of the land. However, they in that land, are all blameworthy if they have not enabled one of them to seek Sharee'ah knowledge in order to remove from themselves the collective obligation of having that knowledge among them. As Allaah, the Most Glorified and the Most Exalted, said ◈ **And it is not proper for the believers to go out to fight Jihaad all together. Of every troop of them, a party only should go forth, that they (who are left behind) may get instructions in Islamic religion, and that they may warn their people when they return to them, so that they may beware of evil.** ◈ – (Surah at-Tawbah: 122)*

[3]   Taken from bazmool.net

Similarly, we should know the importance of referring to reliable students of knowledge from the lands of the Muslims, *"May Allaah increase you in goodness, the questioner says: due to the fact that we do not have scholars or students of knowledge in our country, some of the people have undertaken calling by telephone and through other means some of those students of knowledge or recommended by the scholars in order to benefit from them. Is this something which is prohibited?"* Sheikh Muhammad Baazmol, responded saying,

"All praise is due to Allaah, praise and good mention be upon the Messenger of Allaah, and upon his household, his Companions, and all those who follow them. The practice of calling students of knowledge and calling the scholars in order to ask and gain clarity from them is from those essential matters related to your religion. In fact, this may be from those matters which are obligatory.

Since it times it will not be possible for person to seek sound knowledge of different issues except through asking such questions. This is clear because Allaah, the Most Perfect and the Most High, stated, ❧...so ask the people of the Reminder if you do not know. ❧-(Surah al-Anbiyaa': 7)"

The guiding scholar Sheikh al-'Utheimeen, may Allaah have mercy upon him, clarified that, even when we do not always see the benefit or result conveying reminders with good manners and in the proper way- it is still important, [4]

"It is necessary that reminders about what is correct be made, even when you believe that reminder may not benefit others, as it will benefit you when your intention is to convey and inform the people that such and such matter which you have mentioned is obligatory, or something prohibited.

Otherwise if you simply remained silent the people would enter and engage in that prohibited matter. This is because the general people say, [If this was something prohibited for Muslims then the scholars would mention it.] or [If this was something obligatory for Muslims then the scholars would mention it.]

For this reason it is necessary that reminders be put forth. It is required that the guidance of the Sharee'ah be spread whether that outwardly seems to benefit or does not seem to benefit."

The guiding scholar 'Abdul-Lateef Ibn 'Abdur-Rahman Aal-Sheikh, may Allaah have mercy upon him, said, [5]

"Strive in seeking knowledge and teaching it to others, and inviting to the religion of Allaah and His straight path, as you stand in an age where knowledge is being lost, and ignorance has increased and is spread. It is an age when the religion is being altered and replaced,

---

[4]   From his explanation and commentary of Juz' Amma pg. 123
[5]   ad-Durrur as-Sunneeyah vol. 1 pg. 495

and the established practices of the Sunnah are being changed, especially the very foundations of the religion of Islaam."

Sheikh Muhammad ibn Ramzaan al-Haajiree,[6] may Allaah preserve him, said,[7]

"This is a tremendous responsibility which you have, oh seeker of knowledge. So it is only proper that you keep this in mind, working to bring goodness and salvation to yourself as well as to your society. You stand as a beacon of goodness and a lamp reflecting guidance to the others around you, with them following you. If what you do is good they will follow you in that, whereas if you do other than that, then since they still see you as a model to be followed, so be wary and cautious of this."

Imaam al-Bukhaaree, may Allaah have mercy upon him is reported to have said,[8]

"The best of the Muslims is the one who revives the Sunnah of the Messenger of Allaah, may the praise and salutations of Allaah be upon him, which had died. So be patient oh people who were clinging to the practices of the Sunnah, may Allaah have mercy upon you, as certainly you are from the rarest of people."

Imaam 'Abdullaah Ibn al-Mubaarak, may Allaah have mercy upon him, from the leaders of knowledge in the first generations of Islaam said, 'Sufyaan ath-Thawree wrote to me saying, [9]

"Spread your knowledge, but be warned away from

---

[6]   Sheikh Ahmad an-Najmee, may Allaah have mercy upon him, was asked about various individuals known to be conveying knowledge of Islaam to the Muslims. When asked about the state and level of Sheikh al-Haajiree, said, *"... This one is from the leaders of the people of the Sunnah, this one is."* - Taken from an audio file in the voice of the Sheikh.

[7]   From a lecture "Explanation of the work "The Character of the Scholars of Imaam Al-Aajooree given on 1-18-1440"

[8]   As narrated in 'al-Jaama' al-Akhlaaq ar-Raawee wa Aadaab as-Saamee'a' by Khateeb al-Baghdadee

[9]   Hilyatul-Awleeyah, vol. 7 pg. 70

185

celebrity and renown." '

The guiding scholar Sheikh 'Abdul-Lateef Aal-Sheikh, may Allaah have mercy upon him, conveyed to Sheikh Hamd Ibn 'Ateeq,

> *"It is an obligation upon the one who Allaah has blessed and favored with knowledge and wisdom that he share and spread it among the people, as perhaps Allaah will benefit others through him, and guide at his hands someone who will achieve success and contentment."*

Yet often we also have a questions about how to properly transmit what we have learned from our scholars, both living and those who have died. Sheikh Saaleh al-Fauzaan, may Allaah preserve him was asked, ***"If a person hears that a certain scholar has made such and such a ruling, should they transmit it from the direction or spreading knowledge or must they call that scholar to verify what was said first? We hope for a clarification of this."*** He responded, [10]

> *"If he is sure of the validity of the origin of ruling, is so aware and confident in its source then there is nothing to prevent him from spreading it to those who may need to know it. There is nothing to prevent this. This is from the direction of informing others, not as if he himself is issuing a ruling. This is simply from the direction of transmitting the ruling to others. Yes.*

> *This is done upon the condition that he is confident of the validity of attributing that ruling to that scholar, as well as upon the condition that the one who issued the ruling is capable of issuing rulings in Islaam, and is in fact from those suitable to enter this matter of putting forth rulings. Since it is not the case that every individual who is turned to for ruling or conveying knowledge-related issues is in fact someone truly capable*

---

[10]   From audio file in the voice of the sheikh

of this, no! But that he is actually someone truly suitable and capable of issuing Sharee'ah rulings generally, yes."

The eminent guiding scholar Sheikh Muhammad Nasiruddeen al-Albaanee, may Allaah have mercy upon him, was similarly asked, "***Oh our sheikh, if I have heard from you a response to a specific question directed to you, and at a later time someone asks me this same question. So I answer him knowing that I personally do not possess the knowledge sufficient to answer him, but I answer him based upon your previous answer to this same question or I give the answer of one of the scholars, in doing so have I done anything wrong or sinful?***" He replied, [11]

> *Answer: "We hope that that this will not be something considered sinful for you, however it is not the best way for you. Rather you should say: "I have heard from so-and-so such and such ruling or information.". Because there may emerge from the initially mentioned manner of transmitting, some aspects of harm or corruption that were not intended by the one transmitting the information. The first of them is that the speaker who becomes accustomed to speaking in manner will himself be harmed. This is something which we presently see today with great sorrow and regret. Such that if you hear from Zayd a ruling and from 'Amr a ruling, and from Ahmad a ruling, and so on, yet each individual who is asked regarding this ruling answers the question without attributing his response or knowledge of the issue to the one of originally responded to it. Such that those who asked you regarding it assume, or make an indirect assumption that you - the one who responded are a scholar- and this false perception is a harm and corruption that you may become accustomed to.*

---

[11] From tape number 806 from the tape series 'Gatheringsof Guidance & Light'

Additionally the scope of this harm continues to spread, as the one you responded to afterwards conveys your words to someone else. In this manner this false practice which the Ummah was previous informed of, spreads. Just as was predicted by the Messenger, upon him be Allaah's praise and salutations in the narration which was narrated by both Imaams al-Bukhaaree and Muslim on the authority of 'Abdullah Ibn 'Amr Ibn al-'Aas, may Allaah be pleased with both of them, in which he stated that the Messenger of Allaah, upon him be Allaah's praise and salutations, said: **{I heard Allaah's Apostle saying, "Allaah does not take away the knowledge, by removing it from the chests of the scholars, but He takes it away by means of the death of the scholars. Until when none of the scholars remains, people will take as their guides ignorant people who when asked will give their own rulings without knowledge. So they will go astray and will lead the other people astray.}** [12]. *Therefore due to this we hold that the one who is not a scholar, by rather only someone who is transmitting a matter, that he has a responsibility to mention the source which he is transmitting from."*

The questioner says: This is fine sheikh, and what if you have forgotten the source which you originally heard it from? Is it acceptable if you were just to say I heard from a scholar or read in a book?

Sheikh al-Albaanee replied: "There is no prohibition of only saying this if he has indeed forgotten. But if he only acts as if he has forgotten or pretends not to remember, then transmitting this way is not permissible."

Imaam Ibn Baaz, may Allaah have mercy upon him, very importantly said, [13]

---

[12] Narrated in Saheeh al-Bukhaaree: 100, 7307/ Saheeh Muslim: 4829 / Sunan at-Tirmidhee: 2576/ Sunan Ibn Maajah: 51/ Musnad Of Ahmad: 6222, 6498, 6602/ & Sunan ad-Daaramee: 239 from the hadeeth of 'Abdullah Ibn 'Umar Ibn al-'Aas

[13] Majmu'a al-Fataawa wa Maqalaat, vol. 4 pg. 45

"What is legislated in Islaam is that when a Muslim hears a statement that is of benefit, that he conveys it to others. The same applies to a Muslimah, she should convey to others whatever she hears of sound knowledge. This is due to the statement of the Prophet, may the praise and salutations of Allaah be upon him, "Convey from me even if it is a single statement." And he, may the praise and salutations of Allaah be upon him, if he addressed the people, said, "Let those who are present convey to those who are absent. For perhaps the one to whom it is conveyed will understand it better than the one who first hears it.""

He, may Allaah have mercy upon him, also encouraged us saying, [14]

"A seeker of knowledge should be cognizant and knowledgeable of his religion, as well as one who offers sincere advice to the worshipers for the sake of Allaah. He should stand with his head lifted high, as someone respectable and estimable wherever he may be."

---

[14] Majmu'aal-Fataawa wa Maqalaat, vol. 7 page 238

THE NAKHLAH
EDUCATIONAL SERIES:

MISSION

The Purpose of the 'Nakhlah Educational Series' is to contribute to the present knowledge based efforts which enable Muslim individuals, families, and communities to understand and learn Islaam and then to develop within and truly live Islaam. Our commitment and goal is to contribute beneficial publications and works that:

Firstly, reflect the priority, message and methodology of all the prophets and messengers sent to humanity, meaning that single revealed message which embodies the very purpose of life, and of human creation. As Allaah the Most High has said,

❧ *We sent a Messenger to every nation ordering them that they should worship Allaah alone, obey Him and make their worship purely for Him, and that they should avoid everything worshipped besides Allaah. So from them there were those whom Allaah guided to His religion, and there were those who were unbelievers for whom misguidance was ordained. So travel through the land and see the destruction that befell those who denied the Messengers and disbelieved.* ❧ –(Surah an-Nahl: 36)

Secondly, building upon the above foundation, our commitment is to contributing publications and works which reflect the inherited message and methodology of the acknowledged scholars of the many various branches of Sharee'ah knowledge who stood upon the straight path of preserved guidance in every century and time since the time of our Messenger, may Allaah's praise and salutations be upon him. These people of knowledge, who are the inheritors of the Final Messenger, have always adhered closely to the two revealed sources of guidance: the Book of Allaah and the Sunnah of the Messenger of Allaah- may Allaah's praise and salutations be upon him, upon the united consensus, standing with the body of guided Muslims in every century - preserving and transmitting the true religion generation after generation. Indeed the Messenger of Allaah, may Allaah's praise and salutations be upon him, informed us that, *{ A group of people amongst my Ummah will remain obedient to Allaah's orders. They will not be harmed by those who leave them nor by those who oppose them, until Allaah's command for the Last Day comes upon them while they remain on the right path. }* (Authentically narrated in Saheeh al-Bukhaaree).

The guiding scholar Sheikh Zayd al-Madkhalee, may Allaah protect him, stated in his writing, 'The Well Established Principles of the Way of the First Generations of Muslims: It's Enduring & Excellent Distinct Characteristics' that,

"From among these principles and characteristics is that the methodology of tasfeeyah -or clarification, and tarbeeyah -or education and cultivation- is clearly affirmed and established as a true way coming from the first three generations of Islaam, and is something well known to the people of true merit from among them, as is concluded by considering all the related evidence.

What is intended by tasfeeyah, when referring to it generally, is clarifying that which is the truth from that which is falsehood, what is goodness from that which is harmful and corrupt, and when referring to its specific meanings it is distinguishing the noble Sunnah of the Prophet and the people of the Sunnah from those innovated matters brought into the religion and the people who are supporters of such innovations.

As for what is intended by tarbeeyah, it is calling all of the creation to take on the manners and embrace the excellent character invited to by that guidance revealed to them by their Lord through His worshiper and Messenger Muhammad, may Allaah's praise and salutations be upon him; so that they might have good character, manners, and behavior. As without this they cannot have a good life, nor can they put right their present condition or their final destination. And we seek refuge in Allaah from the evil of not being able to achieve that rectification."

Thus the methodology of the people of standing upon the Prophet's Sunnah, and proceeding upon the 'way of the believers' in every century is reflected in a focus and concern with these two essential matters: tasfeeyah or clarification of what is original, revealed message from the Lord of all the worlds, and tarbeeyah or education and raising of ourselves, our families, and our communities, and our lands upon what has been distinguished to be that true message and path.

The Roles of the Scholars & General Muslims In Raising the New Generation

The priority and focus of the 'Nakhlah Educational Series' is reflected within in the following statements of Sheikh al-Albaanee, may Allaah have mercy upon him:

"As for the other obligation, then I intend by this the education of the young generation upon Islaam purified from all of those impurities we have mentioned, giving them a correct Islamic education from their very earliest years, without any influence of a foreign, disbelieving education."

(Silsilat al-Hadeeth ad-Da'eefah, Introduction page 2.)

"...And since the Messenger of Allaah, may Allaah's praise and salutations be upon him, has indicated that the only cure to remove this state of humiliation that we find ourselves entrenched within, is truly returning back to the religion. Then it is clearly obligatory upon us - through the people of knowledge- to correctly and properly understand the religion in a way that conforms to the sources of the Book of Allaah and the Sunnah, and that we educate and raise a new virtuous, righteous generation upon this."

(Clarification and Cultivation and the Need of the Muslims for Them)

It is essential in discussing our perspective upon this obligation of raising the new generation of Muslims, that we highlight and bring attention to a required pillar of these efforts as indicated by Sheikh al-Albaanee, may Allaah have mercy upon him, and others- in the golden words, "*through the people of knowledge*". Since something we commonly experience today is that many people have various incorrect understandings of the role that the scholars should have in the life of a Muslim, failing to understand the way in which they fulfill their position as the inheritors of the Messenger of Allaah, may Allaah's praise and salutations be upon him, and stand as those who preserve and enable us to practice the guidance of Islaam.

Similarly the guiding scholar Sheikh 'Abdul-'Azeez Ibn Baaz, may Allaah have mercy upon him, also emphasized this same overall responsibility:

"...It is also upon a Muslim that he struggles diligently in that which will place his worldly affairs in a good state, just as he must also strive in the correcting of his religious affairs and the affairs of his own family. As the people of his household have a significant right over him that he strive diligently in rectifying their affair and guiding them towards goodness, due to the statement of Allaah, the Most Exalted, ❲ **Oh you who believe! Save yourselves and your families Hellfire whose fuel is men and stones** ❳ *-(Surah at-Tahreem: 6)*

So it is upon you to strive to correct the affairs of the members of your family. This includes your wife, your children- both male and female- and such as your own brothers. This concerns all of the people in your family, meaning you should strive to teach them the religion, guiding and directing them, and warning them from those matters Allaah has prohibited for us. Because you are the one who is responsible for them as shown in the statement of the Prophet, may Allaah's praise and salutations be upon him, { **Every one of you is a guardian,** *and responsible for what is in his custody. The ruler is a guardian of his subjects and responsible for them; a husband is a guardian of his family and is responsible for it; a lady is a guardian of her husband's house and is responsible for it, and a servant is a guardian of his master's property and is responsible for it....}* Then the Messenger of Allaah, may Allaah's praise and salutations be upon him, continued to say, *{...so all of you are guardians and are responsible for those under your authority.}* (Authentically narrated in Saheeh al-Bukhaaree & Muslim)

It is upon us to strive diligently in correcting the affairs of the members of our families, from the aspect of purifying their sincerity of intention for Allaah's sake alone in all of their deeds, and ensuring that they truthfully believe in and follow the Messenger of Allaah, may Allaah's praise and salutations be upon him, their fulfilling the prayer and the other obligations which Allaah the Most Exalted has commanded for us, as well as from the direction of distancing them from everything which Allaah has prohibited.

It is upon every single man and women to give advice to their families about the fulfillment of what is obligatory upon them. Certainly, it is upon the woman as well as upon the man to perform this. In this way our homes become corrected and rectified in regard to the most important and essential matters. Allaah said to His Prophet, may Allaah's praise and salutations be upon him, ﴿ **And enjoin the ritual prayers on your family...** ﴾ *(Surah Taha: 132) Similarly, Allaah the Most Exalted said to His prophet Ismaa'aeel,* ﴿ **And mention in the Book, Ismaa'aeel. Verily, he was true to what he promised, and he was a Messenger, and a Prophet. And he used to enjoin on his family and his people the ritual prayers and the obligatory charity, and his Lord was pleased with him.** ﴾ *-(Surah Maryam: 54-55)*

As such, it is only proper that we model ourselves after the prophets and the best of people, and be concerned with the state of the members of our households. Do not be neglectful of them, oh worshipper of Allaah! Regardless of whether it is concerning your wife, your mother, father, grandfather, grandmother, your brothers, or your children; it is upon you to strive diligently in correcting their state and condition..."

(Collection of Various Rulings and Statements- Sheikh 'Abdul-'Azeez Ibn 'Abdullah Ibn Baaz, Vol. 6, page 47)

We hope to contribute works which enable every striving Muslim who acknowledges the proper position of the scholars, to fulfill the recognized duty and obligation which lays upon each one of us to bring the light of Islaam into our own lives as individuals as well as into our homes and among our families. Towards this goal we are committed to developing educational publications and comprehensive educational curriculums -through cooperation with and based upon the works of the scholars of Islaam and the students of knowledge. Works which, with the assistance of Allaah, the Most High, we can utilize to educate and instruct ourselves, our families and our communities upon Islaam in both principle and practice. The publications and works of the Nakhlah Educational Series are divided into the following categories:

Basic: Ages 4- 6

Elementary: Ages 6-11

Secondary: Ages 11-14

High School: Ages 14- Young Adult

General: Young Adult –Adult

Supplementary: All Ages

Publications and works within these stated levels will, with the permission of Allaah, encompass different beneficial areas and subjects, and will be offered in every permissible form of media and medium. As certainly, as the guiding scholar Sheikh Saaleh Fauzaan al-Fauzaan, may Allaah preserve him, has stated,

"Beneficial knowledge is itself divided into two categories. Firstly is that knowledge which is tremendous in its benefit, as it benefits in this world and continues to benefit in the Hereafter. This is religious Sharee'ah knowledge. And secondly, that which is limited and restricted to matters related to the life of this world, such as learning the processes of manufacturing various goods. This is a category of knowledge related specifically to worldly affairs.

…As for the learning of worldly knowledge, such as knowledge of manufacturing, then it is legislated upon us collectively to learn whatever the Muslims have a need for. Yet If they do not have a need for this knowledge, then learning it is a neutral matter upon the condition that it does not compete with or displace any areas of Sharee'ah knowledge…"

("Explanations of the Mistakes of Some Writers", Pages 10-12)

We ask Allaah, the most High to bless us with success in contributing to the many efforts of our Muslim brothers and sisters committed to raising themselves as individuals and the next generation of our children upon that Islaam which Allaah has perfected and chosen for us, and which He has enabled the guided Muslims to proceed upon in each and every century. We ask him to forgive us, and forgive the Muslim men and the Muslim women, and to guide all the believers to everything He loves and is pleased with. The success is from Allaah, The Most High The Most Exalted, alone and all praise is due to Him.

Abu Sukhailah Khalil Ibn-Abelahyi
Taalib al-Ilm Educational Resources

30 Days of Guidance [Book 1]: Learning Fundamental Principles of Islaam

A Short Journey Within the Work Al-Ibaanah al-Sughrah With Sheikh 'Abdul-'Azeez Ibn 'Abdullah ar-Raajhee

AUTHOR - COMPILER - TRANSLATOR

Abu Sukhailah Khalil Ibn-Abelahyi

BOOK OVERVIEW

- Interactive course book
- Focused upon both beliefs & principles
- 1st book in 30 Day Series

WHO IS THIS BOOK FOR

All age levels

For every Muslim who wishes to live their life in a way pleasing to Allaah it is essential that they ensure that their beliefs and practices actually have evidence and support from within the sources of Islaam. This work approaches this challenge in a way that allows an individual to proceed through discussions related to this a day at a time over thirty days, based upon explanations from one of today's noble scholars.

WHAT YOU WILL LEARN IN THIS BOOK

Related to essential basic principles of guidance

The role of Islaam in today's world is something which is indisputable and often contested. There are many different understandings of Islaam which range from dangerous extremism, all the way to vulnerable laxity. Yet our well-known scholars continue to work diligently in openly examining and clarifying the false ideas and practices that are attributed to Islaam.

PRICING

- *Hardcover -USD $45.00*
- *Soft cover -USD $27.50*
- *Kindle -USD $09.99*

PDF PREVIEW

https://ilm4.us/30daybook1

PURCHASE BOOK

http://taalib.com/4134

30 Days of Guidance [Book 2]: Cultivating The Character & Behavior of Islaam

A Short Journey Within The Work Al-Adab Al-Mufrad With Sheikh Zayd Ibn Muhammad Ibn Haadee al-Madkhalee

AUTHOR - COMPILER - TRANSLATOR

Abu Sukhailah Khalil Ibn-Abelahyi

BOOK OVERVIEW

*   Interactive course book
*   Focused upon both character & behavior
*   2nd book in 30 Day Series

WHO IS THIS BOOK FOR

All age levels

This course book is intended for the Muslim individual for self-study, as well as for us as Muslim parents in our essential efforts to educate our children within Islaam and our ongoing endeavor of cultivating them upon the extraordinary character and behavior of our beloved Prophet. It is also intended to be an easy to use classroom resource for our Muslim teachers in the every growing numbers of Islamic centers...

WHAT YOU WILL LEARN IN THIS BOOK

Related to the subject of perfecting ones character

Some of the questions that this course book helps us answer are: Are you prepared for your reckoning? Are you always working for good while you can? Do you remember the benefit in your difficulties? Is your life balanced as was the lives of the Companions? How do you deal with your own faults and those of others? Do you know what things bring you closer to Jannah?....and more

PRICING

*   *Hardcover -USD $45.00*
*   *Soft cover -USD $27.50*
*   *Kindle -USD $09.99*

PDF PREVIEW

https://ilm4.us/30daybook2

PURCHASE BOOK

http://taalib.com/4137

30 Days of Guidance [Book 3]: Signposts Towards Rectification & Repentance

A Short Journey through Selected Questions & Answers with
Sheikh Muhammad Ibn Saaleh al-'Utheimeen

AUTHOR - COMPILER - TRANSLATOR

Abu Sukhailah Khalil Ibn-Abelahyi

BOOK OVERVIEW

- Interactive course book
- Focused upon both change & growth in Islaam
- 3rd book in 30 Day Series

WHO IS THIS BOOK FOR

All age levels

This course book is intended for any Muslim who wishes to improve his life and rectify his heart. Yet this self rectification or purification of the soul must be done in the correct way and upon the correct foundation of knowledge from the Sunnah, if it is to lead to true success in both this life and the next. Ibn al-Qayyim, may Allaah have mercy upon him, also stated, 'The true purification of the soul and the self is directly connected to those messengers sent to humanity..."

WHAT YOU WILL LEARN IN THIS BOOK

Related to the Subject of perfecting ones character

This course discusses in detail the inward and outward changes and steps we must take as striving Muslims to improve and bring our lives into a better state after mistakes, sins, slips, and negligence. Discussing real life problems and issues faced by Muslim of all ages and situations -the Sheikh advises and indicates the road to reform, repentance, and true rectification.

PRICING

- *Hardcover -USD $45.00*
- *Soft cover -USD $27.50*
- *Kindle -USD $09.99*

PDF PREVIEW

https://ilm4.us/30daybook3

PURCHASE BOOK

http://taalib.com/4150

Foundations For The New Muslim & Newly Striving Muslim

A Short Journey through Selected Questions & Answers with
Sheikh 'Abdul-'Azeez Ibn 'Abdullah Ibn Baaz

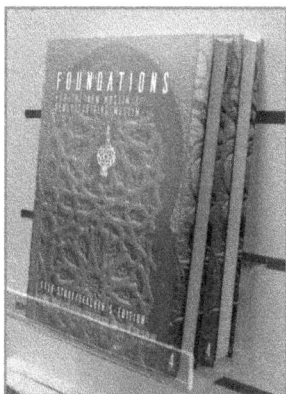

AUTHOR - COMPILER - TRANSLATOR

Abu Sukhailah Khalil Ibn-Abelahyi

BOOK OVERVIEW

- Interactive course book
- Focused upon essential beliefs & challenges
- 4th book in 30 Day Series

WHO IS THIS BOOK FOR

All age levels

This course book is intended for both the person who has newly embraced Islaam or that Muslim or Muslimah whom Allaah has blessed to now have the resolve within themselves to truly turn towards their Most Merciful Lord and commit themselves to becoming a better worshipper upon knowledge. It for that individual who, regardless of the direction they came from, wishes to change both the inward and outward aspects of their lives to now move in a direction truly pleasing to Allaah.

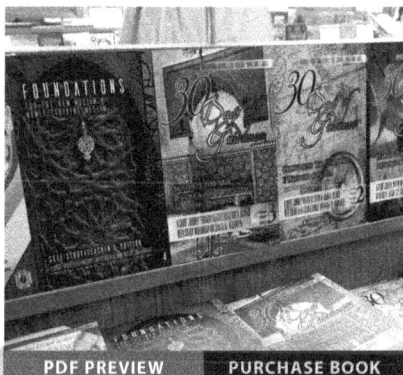

WHAT YOU WILL LEARN IN THIS BOOK

Related to building a firm foundation for our Islaam

This course book discusses What are the conditions of correct Islaam? Is faith only what is in our hearts? When is it necessary for me to ask a scholar? What is the guidance of Islaam about our health? What should I do after falling into sin again and again? Do I have to make up for my previous negligence? How should I interact with the non-Muslims I know? and more...

PRICING

- *Hardcover -USD $45.00*
- *Soft cover -USD $27.50*
- *Kindle -USD $09.99*

PDF PREVIEW

PURCHASE BOOK

https://ilm4.us/30daybook4   http://taalib.com/4147

Statements of the Guiding Scholars of Our Age Regarding Books & their Advice to the Beginner Seeker of Knowledge

[Contains A List of over 300 Books Recommended By The Scholars In The Various Sciences Of Islaam]

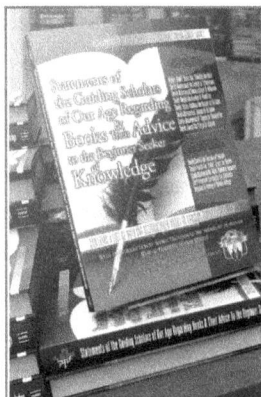

AUTHOR - COMPILER - TRANSLATOR

Abu Sukhailah Khalil Ibn-Abelahyi

BOOK OVERVIEW

- Taken from words of senior scholars
- Provides road map for Sharee'ah study
- Divided into seven main sections

WHO IS THIS BOOK FOR

All age levels

A comprehensive guidebook for the Muslim who wishes to learn about his or her religion with the proper goal and aim, in the proper way, and through the proper books. This question and answer book is for those who seek advice from some of the senior scholars of the current century regarding seeking knowledge, against books containing misguidance.

WHAT YOU WILL LEARN IN THIS BOOK

Sources and subjects of seeking Sharee'ah knowledge

This book is intended to enable any sincere Muslim to strive to proceed with correct methods and manners in seeking of beneficial knowledge for themselves and in order to guide their families. The scholars are the carriers of authentic knowledge and the inheritors of the Messenger of Allaah. Their explantations make clear for us the way to learn and then live Islaam.

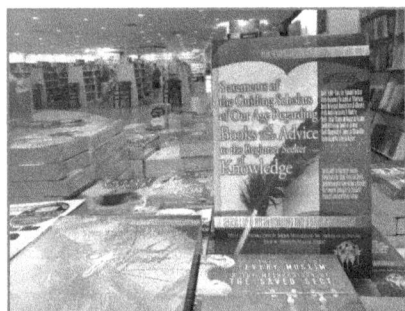

PRICING

- *Hardcover -USD $45.00*
- *Soft cover -USD $27.50*
- *Kindle -USD $09.99*

PDF PREVIEW

https://ilm4.us/seeker

PURCHASE BOOK

http://taalib.com/79

An Educational Course Based Upon Beneficial Answers to Questions On Innovated Methodologies

of Sheikh Saaleh Ibn Fauzaan al-Fauzaan

AUTHOR - COMPILER - TRANSLATOR

Abu Sukhailah Khalil Ibn-Abelahyi

BOOK OVERVIEW

* Interactive course book
* Focuses upon principles of the straight path
* Discusses modern groups and movements

WHO IS THIS BOOK FOR

All age levels

This course book is for any Muslim who wishes to understand the detailed guiding principles of Islaam as discussed by the scholars throughout the centuries, including the scholars of our age. These principles were initially put in place and practiced by the generation of the Companions of the Messenger of Allaah, may Allaah be pleased with all of them, when Islaam was first established, and have been implemented in each and every century by those Muslims following in their noble footsteps.

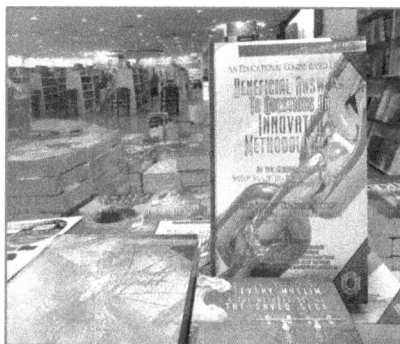

WHAT YOU WILL LEARN IN THIS BOOK

Related to the detailed way we understand Islaam

This course focuses upon the importance of clarity in the way you understand and practice Islaam. What is the right way or methodology to do so? Examine the evidences and proofs from the sources texts of the Qur'aan and Sunnah and the statements of many scholars explaining them, that connect you directly to the Islaam of the Messenger of Allaah.

PRICING

* *Hardcover -USD $50*
* *Soft cover -USD $32.50*
* *Kindle -USD $09.99*

PDF PREVIEW

http://ilm4.us/minhaj

PURCHASE BOOK

http://taalib.com/4144

The Belief of Every Muslim & The Methodology of The Saved Sect

Lessons & Benefits From the Two Excellent Works of Sheikh Muhammad Ibn Jameel Zaynoo

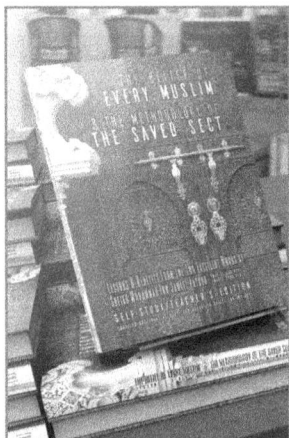

AUTHOR - COMPILER - TRANSLATOR

Abu Sukhailah Khalil Ibn-Abelahyi

BOOK OVERVIEW

- Interactive course book with diagrams
- Discusses how to study and from whom
- Focuses upon both beliefs & practices

WHO IS THIS BOOK FOR

All age levels

This course book is for any Muslim who is looking for an easy-to-follow course- based discussion of not only what it is important to learn but also concise advice on how to study and learn Islaam. Taking selections from two well-known books of Sheikh Zaynoo, may Allaah have mercy upon him, it offers an overview of some of the characteristics and hallmarks which distinguished that clear call our beloved Prophet brought to humanity.

WHAT YOU WILL LEARN IN THIS BOOK

Related to foundation of Islaam & gaining knowledge

This Islamic studies course discusses the different levels of knowledge, important matters related to seeking knowledge, essential study skills, the role of evidence in Islaam, differing and taking from the scholars. Addditionally, it explains the central role that the foundation that worshipping Allaah alone should have in our lives, and how that distinguishes every single person.

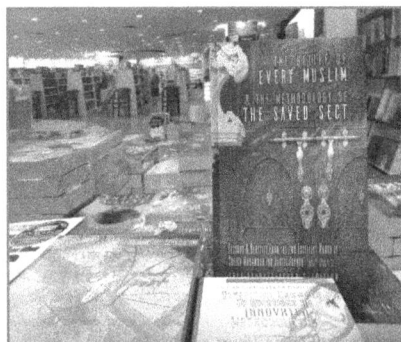

PRICING

- *Hardcover -USD $45.00*
- *Soft cover -USD $30*
- *Kindle -USD $09.99*

PDF PREVIEW

https://ilm4.us/savedsect

PURCHASE BOOK

http://taalib.com/4141

The Cure, The Explanation, The Clear Affair, & The Brilliantly Distinct Signpost

Book 1: Sources of Islaam & The Way of the Companions- *A Course Upon Commentaries of Usul as-Sunnah' of Imaam Ahmad*

AUTHOR - COMPILER - TRANSLATOR

Abu Sukhailah Khalil Ibn-Abelahyi

BOOK OVERVIEW

* Interactive course book with 15 lessons
* Focuses upon sources & principles of Islaam
* First book in continuing series

WHO IS THIS BOOK FOR

All age levels

This course book is intended for any Muslim who wishes to connect himself to our beloved Prophet. inwardly and outwardly, in order to walk in his footsteps upon knowledge as a worshiper of Allaah. It is designed to help you, as a Muslim, identify the correct sources, principles, and beliefs of the evidenced methodology of Islaam upon scholarship and proofs, in order to be able to distinguished what opposes them from incorrect sources, principles, and false beliefs.

WHAT YOU WILL LEARN IN THIS BOOK

Related to the independent sources of Sharee'ah guidance

This course book discusses the universal nature and correct beliefs about Islaam as a revealed religion. It also discusses specifically what are the correct evidenced beliefs held by the people of adherence to the Sunnah throughout the centuries about the nature of the Qur'aan, the Sunnah and scholarly Consensus.

PRICING

* *Hardcover -USD $45.00*
* *Soft cover -USD $30*
* *Kindle -USD $09.99*

PDF PREVIEW

https://ilm4.us/usulbook1

PURCHASE BOOK

http://taalib.com/62874